FIRST 32 WORDS OF SAPIENS

Volume II, Part 1

Shaktybek Imashov

Copyright © 2024 Shaktybek Imashov

All rights reserved

No part of this book may be reproduced, or stored in a retrieval system, or transmitted in any form or by any means, electronic, mechanical, photocopying, recording, or otherwise, without express written permission of the publisher.

ISBN: 9798342623575

Cover design by: Art Painter
Library of Congress Control Number: 2018675309
Printed in the United States of America

CONTENTS

Title Page
Copyright
Introduction
WE STARTED FROM IMITATIONS   1
THE FIRST WORDS   11
FURTHER EVOLUTION   35
LITERACY VS. ORALITY   53
ORAL MIND   63
"THE KYRGYZ ROOTS" OF THE BURNING MAN, ALEXANDER'S IDEAL SOCIETY, AND EGYPTIAN MYTHS   93
BIBLIOGRAPHY   109
LIST OF SOURCES FOR IMAGES: 111
NOTES   115
About The Author   123

INTRODUCTION

This book is the first part of the second volume in the Proto- Yoga series. By examining specific linguistic features of the Kyrgyz language, it aims to reconstruct humanity's earliest "vocabulary" of single-sound morphemes. This reconstructed linguistic "toolkit" is then applied to decipher ancient terms, continuing the exploration of cultural and linguistic interconnectedness between ancient civilizations, a theme from the previous volume.

As a continuation of the series, this book incorporates the explanatory notes outlined in the *Structure of The Exploration* chapter of Volume I. For a comprehensive understanding, readers are encouraged to consult this chapter, available for preview in the e-book version of Volume I on Amazon.

A Key Note on Translations (See the *Structure of The Exploration*):

Unless otherwise specified, English translations of Kyrgyz words are derived from their Russian equivalents as presented in K. Yudahin's dictionary.

To ensure clarity and accuracy, the following referencing conventions apply:

- **Single Meaning:** If a Kyrgyz word has only one listed meaning in Yudahin's dictionary, no reference number is provided for its translation.

- **Multiple Meanings:** When a Kyrgyz word has multiple meanings, references to the specific meaning within a particular context are indicated as follows:
  - **First Listed Meaning:** Translations without a reference number correspond to the initial meaning listed in the dictionary.
  - **Multiple Definitions:** Bracketed numbers following a translation signify additional or indirect meanings. The corresponding endnote provides further clarification.

WE STARTED FROM IMITATIONS

Viewed as a technology, literacy is often equated with civilization, representing an advancement that has shaped our modern world.

However, before the emergence of written language, there long existed an oral form of communication that holds the origins of human culture itself.

Caption of the Chapter Opening Image (Fig. 1): *Manaschi*—the Oral Historian (Source: Public Domain. See List of Figures)

The *Manaschi*, a skilled oral storyteller, narrates the epic Manas with captivating facial expressions and expressive body language, bringing the legendary tale to life.

Charles Darwin's assertion (Darwin, 56) that *"language owes its origin to the imitation and modification, aided by signs and gestures, of various natural sounds, the voices of other animals, and man's own instinctive cries"* hints at the multifaceted nature of early language. It was more than a mere collection of sounds; it was a complex interplay of sounds and gestures, utilizing the tools available to our embodied minds. In this light, orality, juxtaposed against the visual but static nature of literacy, emerges as the articulation of thoughts, buoyed by bodily expressions. An intriguing embodiment of this idea is found in the delivery of the Kyrgyz epic Manas (Fig. 1 above). Its fluidity mirrors its origin beyond the confines of script, highlighting the nuanced technology that is orality.

The idea of language emerging from the imitation of various sounds in nature also resonates vividly in the Kyrgyz language, which has a very rich representation of sound mimicry. This resonance is exemplified by the language's remarkable abundance of expressive onomatopoeias, a feature emphasized by K. Yudahin in the description of his Kyrgyz-Russian dictionary (Yudahin, 8). I myself encountered over 267 words in Yudahin's dictionary only marked as imitative, and there are many others categorized differently but are onomatopoeias in their nature [1].

These onomatopoeias not only endure in the language, providing symbolic depth, but are also distinctly identifiable as the root of other words.

For instance, the exclamation *oŭ!* [oj], akin to English *oh!* or *oops!*, signifies surprise. Its brevity and multifaceted meanings vividly illustrate its connection to the primordial vocabulary. Beyond being an onomatopoeia expressing the *sudden* and *unexpected occurrence* of something, it has evolved into various terms. It can be a noun referring to a *cavity* in the Earth's surface, perhaps linked to exclamations (*oŭ!*) uttered after accidental falls into such holes. Additionally, it functions as a verb meaning *to hollow out*, referring to the creation of traps for prey in the form of that *oŭ* cavity. Furthermore, it takes on a more abstract sense, representing a *thought* or mental process, possibly connected to the contemplative state experienced while trapped in such cavities (*оӊ*). Consequently, it serves as the progenitor of a multitude of derivatives.

Another Kyrgyz imitative word *аж* [adʒ] conveys the notion of aggressive shouting or yelling. From this root emerges the derivative *ажа* [adʐa], which translates to a senior person, carrying the connotation of someone who holds the right to raise their voice at others. This term appears among the 27 words of the common proto-human vocabulary (discussed in the Volume I) with a similar meaning of *mother, older female relative*. Interestingly, in the context of a senior and older person, the term resembles the English word *age*. While the origin of *age* is assumed to be from Vulgar Latin, the phonetic similarity between *age* and *ажа* or *аж* is more striking than with the suggested *aetāticum [2].

Onomatopoeia *бур* [bur], which also functions as a verb (to) *turn*. When considered as an imitative word, it conjures imagery of *ashes, dust,* or *aroma rising*. This term finds resonance in the proto-human language as well, with its meaning in the proto-language *BUR assumed to be *ashes* or *dust*. The immediate derivative of this stem in Kyrgyz is the verb *бура* [bura], which means (to) *emit scent* or (to) *screw*. This stem is notably present in the Kyrgyz verb *буркура* [burqura], which translates as (to) *exude aroma*.

Consider the sound *э* [e], which in Kyrgyz language represent the imitation of the *shortest possible speech sound* and had also evolved to the verb signifying the *existence* itself. This verb is not only a notable root in many Kyrgyz words but also shares linguistic connection with the ancient Latin word for existence, *essentia,* or even the Proto-Indo-European root **es* for *to be* [33]. This connection is further reflected in the Kyrgyz philosophical term эс [es] for *mind/consciousness*—a topic we will explore in more detail in the relevant chapter.

Kyrgyz use the onomatopoeia *ку* [qu] from the "bird language" to summon or land a raptor. It is clearly evident in such words as *куш* [quş] (meaning *a big bird* in general) and philosophical *Kym/Kut*, which represent *all possible Goodness in life* (as discussed in Volume I).

The linguistic connection between imitative sounds and their meanings highlights the profound interplay between language and the natural world. It underscores how imitation played a crucial role in the early development of human communication, allowing our ancestors to convey complex concepts and experiences through imitative sounds and words.

The Kyrgyz language, with its unique proto-linguistic features, offers a fascinating window into the early stages of word formation.

Let's explore some of these intriguing characteristics:

The Short Vowels

In the early stages of human language development, it is reasonable to assume that 'vocabulary' primarily consisted of vowels, easily producible short sounds articulated without obstructing airflow in the vocal tract. The notion of vowels as fundamental sounds produced by human speech organs is reflected in the Latin root of the term *vowel*, which denotes *a sound related to the voice* [3] or *a sound that can be produced by humans using speech* organs [43]. Today, many languages still employ single-vowel morphemes as onomatopoeias or even meaningful words.

Here are examples of such single-phoneme vowel terms from Kyrgyz, notably, each each possessing a remarkably broad, or even a range of meanings:

- *a* [a]: Symbolizes a beginning/initiation of something [39] or is used as an exclamation to denote surprise.

- * э* [e]: Represents the *shortest speech sound* or signifies *existence*.

- *u* [i]: Serves as a questioning exclamation like *so?!*

- *o* [ɒ]: Means *yond*, and *afterlife*.

- *y* [y]: Is used to imitate an *easiest to produce speech sound*, likely due to the narrowest lip position required for its articulation.

Prolonged Vowels

A further embryonic evolutionary phenomenon also preserved in Kyrgyz language. It involves a reversal in the meaning of the root words through the prolonged pronunciation of their vowels, offering a glimpse into the early evolution of language.

For instance, the above mentioned discouraging exclamation *И!?* [i] can be transformed into the affirmative *Ии/Ииу* [ï/iji] by lengthening the vowel [8].

Similarly, the desire expression *Ama!* [ata] (40) becomes the pitiful *Amaa...* [ata] when the final vowel is prolonged

[5].

The verb э and its prolonged form ээ [ë] provide another example of this transformative shift. The meaning *to exist* [6] evolves into the question word *is?* [7]. In another usage, ээ denotes concepts like *to have, control, God,* and *owner,* encapsulating the notion of exercising authority over existence.

Similarly, the pronoun *o* [o], meaning *over there in vicinity,* typically in reference to object *over/on the ground.* When prolonged to *oo* [o:], however, its meaning transforms into the opposed *far away there* and the verb *to cross over.* This suggests a shift from an object being *visible* and *over* the ground to one that has moved *out of sight, beyond and behind* something or the horizon. This process finds parallels in modern English, where phrases like *Oh, no!* can be reversed in meaning by changing them to *Ooh, yes!*

Moreover, while *γ* [y] signifies *narrowness,* its prolonged counterpart *γγ/γзγ* [ygy] ([8]) denotes the action of crumbling, which is the act of spreading *(broadening)* crumbs.

The true power of this remarkable invention by our early common ancestors in primordial linguistics is demonstrated through a pair of words in the Kyrgyz language: *тур* [tur], meaning *to stand,* and *туура* [türa], meaning *a stand* (as in a perch for a raptor, the ancient roots of which was discussed in the Volume I). Notably, the extended pronunciation of the vowel [u] in this case served to differentiate between the process of standing and the object on which one stands. In some languages, this feature was eventually replaced by the use of affixes. This shift can be observed in Russian, where *stay* is *стой* [stoy], and the word for *a stand* becomes *стойка* [stoyka].

Curiously, this linguistic feature that is still present in the Kyrgyz language bears intriguing resemblance to Sanskrit's Vedic period vowel gradation system, particularly in relation to its first and second grades for open vowels [83]. This alignment points to a broader linguistic correlation and highlights the presence of this phenomenon across different languages from ancient times. In fact, this alteration of stem sounds has been integral to the reconstruction of archaic languages such as Proto-Indo-European (PIE).

In the broader context of language development, the linguistic phenomenon described above can be viewed as an early stage in the evolution of verbal language. This phenomenon encompasses the initial emergence of single-vowel morphemes as the first word-like sounds of humanity and the subsequent development of their extended derivatives. It offers a glimpse into an embryonic form of word formation, representing an elemental technique within the realm of human language evolution.

The unique and nascent process of word formation serves as a testament to the Kyrgyz language's suitable role in unraveling the origins and intricacies of linguistic expression. Through this lens, the language becomes a valuable linguistic artifact that not only bridges linguistic history but also offers a remarkable window into the dawn of human communication.

The Clicks

The next step in the evolution of humanity's embryonic vocabulary naturally involves the emergence of another linguistic element that in Kyrgyz language today is only used as a standalone speech unit: *the click sound* [85].

While these sounds might not be explicitly documented in formal dictionaries, some persist in the Kyrgyz language. Beyond [ǂ] ([9]), previously discussed in Volume I, there is another one [k'] that, when pronounced in sequence, serves as onomatopoeia designed to sooth the animals [10].

Being easily produced [84], as evidenced by the ability of creatures with less developed vocal tracts, such as dolphins and even crabs [86], to produce similar sounds, clicks would naturally represent the next stage in the development of human speech organs.

Interestingly, some of the click-rich languages in South Africa, which possibly have the world's richest array of phonemes, are also notably rich in consonants [11]. This richness might be attributed to the abundant sources of similar sounds available in the languages' natural environments.

In the journey of our progenitors northward, the number of click sounds naturally diminished, aligning with the changes in their new environment.

A "Creaky""K"

Another fascinating linguistic phenomenon preserved in the Kyrgyz language, possibly tracing back to humanity's earliest forms of speech, is the laryngeal quality of the phoneme к [q]. As discussed in Volume I, this guttural pronunciation was also attested in pre-Ancient Greek Hittite, suggesting a deep-rooted connection between early language systems. The laryngeal sound may represent a transitional stage in speech development, bridging the gap between primordial click sounds and more refined consonants. This hypothesis is supported by the phone's ability, as discussed in the Volume I, to shift depending on the vowel it is paired with, transforming into [k], [g], [ɣ], [χ], or [ʁ]. Such variations reflect the diverse range of sounds, preserved in Kyrgyz of today, that may have originated from a common linguistic ancestor, underscoring the dynamic evolution of human speech from its earliest forms [12].

The Consonants

Presumably, the early human ability to produce vowels and click sounds led to efforts to combine them, giving rise to the new form of the speech sound that this time is articulated with complete or partial closure of the vocal tract—the *consonants* [44]. The assumption on the sequence of their origination is grounded in the natural constraint of pronouncing consonants on their own, a constraint reflected in the core meaning of the term itself [15] and in the majority of alphabets where consonants are accompanied by vowels. This quality of consonants is also notable in the authentic Kyrgyz vocabulary, where some of them can't initiate a word or, rather, the words they initiate, as will be discussed later, are "prefixed" by certain vowels.

The Compound Form

Regardless, we now observe the introduction of words composed of vowels and consonants as the second major speech sound component, in addition to the single-vowel terms (with some use of prolonged counterpart and click sounds of course) in the proto-human language. From this point, speech becomes more complex, evolving into a combination of a vowel and a consonant, where each component carries a primordial morphemic, very broad meaning. This developmental process has left discernible traces, as evidenced by the abundance of such two-phoneme terms in Kyrgyz.

Indeed, a plethora of such Kyrgyz root words, ranging from *аж* [adʒ] to *ак* [aq], *ку* [qu], *ур* [ur], *эл* [el], has already come to the forefront in Volume I, and more are poised to be unveiled throughout the course of this book. Identifying these terms as pivotal elements in the development of an early language, we can view them as closed compound words formed from single-vowel and single-consonant stems. This perspective offers a unique opportunity to explore the connotations that our distant ancestors embedded in the earliest segments of human speech. These individual sounds, now recognized as phonemes—the building blocks of words—once functioned as single-sound morphemes or word-like entities in primitive verbal communication. It is logical to assume that these foundational units of speech carried broad, context-dependent meanings, shaping the way early humans conveyed ideas.

THE FIRST WORDS

By delving into the vocabulary of our proto-human lexicon, we can further enrich our understanding of the pivotal roles that phonemes, both as consonants and vowels, played within these foundational terms and how their significance has cascaded down through the annals of linguistic evolution.

Some of these one-phoned stems, as encountered before, are still well existing in Kyrgyz language, while others can be deduced from it, again showcasing its ability to preserve features from the proto-language.

Caption of the Chapter Opening Image (Fig. 2): View of the Highland Valley in Switzerland, reminiscent of the typical Kyrgyz landscapes. (Source: Public Domain. See List of Figures)

Glacial meltwater, flowing down from the white snow covered picks, is a primary source of mountain rivers, as illustrated in this image.

Word-Like Phonemes

An illustrative example of such linguistic extraction can be found in Kyrgyz term *ак* [aq], which carries the dual meaning, being *to flow* as a verb and *white* or *pure* as an adjective. Considering the Kyrgyz people's historic mountainous environment similar to the one depicted Fig. 2, a possible underlying concept embedded in this dual meaning might be 'the *white* substance that *purifies* and *flows* downward from *high above* toward us.'

In the context of Kyrgyz nature such a substance would be snow that covers mountain summits and transforms into water upon melting. Remarkably, this concept resonates with the Latin root word *aqua*.

Based on this perspective, the deeper proto-connotation of the term *a* [a] can be inferred as referring to something that is *distant, elevated,* and *pure*. The connotation that that suggests *extreme visibility*, representing the concept of being *distinct, above, prominent,* the *first to be seen*.

Such a quality of the phoneme [a] is also notable in the English words *up* and *upfront*, where it also conveys the idea of elevation and being first/ before something.

The above interpretation of the morpheme [a] is observed in other Kyrgyz two-phoned words as well. For instance, the term *aŭ* [aj], being an exclamation accompanying action of *raising a hand up to attract someone's attention* and also being a noun signifying *moon*, can be linked to what is *first openly visible* and *set apart all* in the sky. Interestingly, this combination of phonemes in English forms the word *eye*, which denotes the *organ* of *vision*, and is also present in terms like *sky* and *high*, both of which carry meanings reminiscent of the interpretation provided.

This intriguing perspective allows us to understand deeper the origins of some other words in modern languages too. For instance, the English term *I*, which sounds exactly as Kyrgyz *aй* from above, could be rooted in the idea of oneself being perceived as *separate from the rest* —*visible first* and *foremost, above all* else. This interpretation suggests that the concept of the human ego has been a fundamental quality present since primordial time.

Similarly, the archaic English form *thy* might signify someone who, among others, is the *most visible* or *prominent* than others. In German, the word *ein* [ajn], meaning *one*, could be seen as denoting something that is the *first visible* or *singular*. These interpretations highlight how linguistic elements from humanity's common ancestral languages can provide insights into the subtle nuances and origins of contemporary vocabulary.

If a two-phoneme word is considered a compound term, where one of part corresponds to an existing single-sound word (such as *a* [a] in Kyrgyz), it becomes easier to infer the potential meaning of the second morpheme.

Thus, the correspondence of the sound [q], which in Kyrgyz language can interchange with [k], [h] or [g] depending on certain rules, within the "proto-connotation" of *ак* [aq] from above, it would refer to a *place* where the melted snow flows. Logically. this would imply the *vicinity* or *land within one's reach*.

This is clearly validated from the derived verb surfaced before—*ку* [qu] (in Volume I), within which it denotes a *place* next to the falconer where the prey bird is being called to. Other ones are *кел* [kel] with the connotation '(to) come to *our place*, '*кал* [qal]—'remain at *our place*, 'and *кир* [gir] —'enter *our place*. 'The latter word, having noun and adjective meanings of *dirt* and *dirty*, also support the idea with the interpretation of them as being the result of *landing* (near by) or quality that comes from the *place* on the ground (around us).

In English, a similar connotation of [q/k/h] is evident in words like *here*, which has its origin in PIE *ke* [qe], and *come* (seen as *arrive at our place*). Moreover, the term *clay* in English, denoting *dirt of earth*, bears connection with the Kyrgyz phoneme [q], same as Sumerian *Ki* with its meaning of *earth* or *land* and the name for the Goddess [13].

Clay, suggested to be from the PIE root meaning *glue/ slime* [14], in addition to the phoneme [k] also contains [l]. In Kyrgyz, the two-phoned terms with phoneme [l] often convey connotations of *being permanently located/ attached to*. This can be observed in the words like ал [al] meaning *(to) take (from)*, which could be decoded as '*elevate* [a] + to *attach* [l] (to yourself).' Here, [a] corresponds to making the object *up*, and [l] as *attaching to yourself* implies that the taken object will stick to you for a long time, suggesting a connotation of '*a permanent location.*' Interestingly, besides the linguistic link to the English word *location*, [l] also starts the word *land*.

Another word containing [l], эл [el], translates to *people* and appears to signify' those who *exist* [e] + permanently *connected/glued/attached* [l] to one another.'

Considering the pattern, the previously reviewed "compound words" with the morpheme [l] as one of the stem can be further understood in the following way: кел [kel] —'become *attached* [l] + to *exist* [e] + in this *place* [k],' кал [qal] —'*stick* ([q]) + *up* ([a]) + to this *place* ([q]).'

Another instance of Kyrgyz "easy to decipher" word is эм [em]. This term encompasses a range of meanings such as an imperative mood of the verb *suck* (towards suckling), a *remedy* or *positive effect* and *an effort*. Correspondingly, the compound connotation of these terms can be seen as '*something of a positive effect from...* 'In this case, the term originates from morphemes [e] and [m], where the meaning of the first one is already known.

As [e] signifies *existence*, in reference to mother's milk for the infant it can be understood as connoting *remedy/positive* effect. Thus, as a verb (an "instruction" for a baby to *suck*), the combination of [e]+[m] can be deciphered as a 'take in (your) *existence* from *me*.' In this vein, *me* would be represented by the "morpheme" [m].

The same understanding could be attributed to the noun, *remedy/a positive effect/an effort*, where [e] would refer to 'something good for (your) *existence*' and [m] would mean 'from *me*.' As here the context is much broader than one way "mama's instruction to the baby" limited to the 'from me to you' dynamic, it includes all options of 'something from us/you/her/him/them/it for them/me/him/us/it.' Accordingly, we can infer that as a primordial morpheme [m] represent a broader sense of *self*.

This idea is reinforced by the meaning of the reverse combination, мэ [me], meaning '*take it from me/us*.' Here, we see that "compound word" conveys almost the same idea of 'take it from my/our-*self/selves* [m] to *be/exist* [e] with you.'

Notably from above, the insights into the Kyrgyz language can potentially reveal how the phonemes in two-phoned "closed compound words" can be linked to nuanced connotations of their one-phoned "morphemes" representing the Sapiens' "earliest vocabulary" of single sound worlds.

Single Vowel Terms

Furthermore, based on the idea that humanity's initial spoken words were likely imitative vowel sounds, an exploration of the connotations carried by single-vowel morphemes in the Kyrgyz language offers us a glimpse into the even earlier vocabulary of our species. These primitive sounds, rich in meaning and context, lay the foundation for the development of human language.

As previously discussed, the Kyrgyz language retains several single-phoned terms in the form of vowels. While some of these vowels, such as *э* [e] indicating *existence* and *o* [ɒ] meaning *over*, still convey clear and productive meanings that can be observed in the formation of contemporary words, others possess broader connotations and are not as straightforward to decode in modern terms. Examples of these include: *a* [a], which represents *initiation*, *visibility*, an *aerial* or *distant* location, and *purity*; and *u* [i], serving as a questioning exclamation, often equivalent to *'so?!'*

To elucidate the nuanced meanings and broader connotations of these single-vowel morphemes, we can delve into their usage and derivative forms.

In the case of above *a* [a], it is employed to signify a range of concepts. These include *initiation*, as seen in the compound term *'а дегенде'* [a degende], which translates to *"when saying 'a'"* and conveys the meaning of *initially*. *A* is also used to express *what/that*, as in the exclamation of disappointment, *а', кокуй!'* [a kɒkuj], which translates to *'what an annoyance!'* It can denote *that*, particularly highlighting the distant quality when compared to the immediate, as exemplified in *а тыгыл'* [a tygyl], meaning *'not only that.'* Additionally, it also serves as the question word *what?* The correspondence of *a* with pronouns like *wha*t and *tha*t, as well as its role in indicating *initiation*, also suggests that it denotes a sense of *apartness*. Interestingly, this *apartness* potentially links *a* to the English indefinite article *a*.

When we consider the above connotations alongside the previously discussed ones, the morpheme [a] emerges as a symbol for the concept of being *first, before, above, in front* and *apart* of all or *the most*. This aligns perfectly with the meaning of the Ancient Greek word *Alpha*, which derives from the even more ancient Phoenician *aleph*.

Remarkably, the modern Kyrgyz word for *Alpha/aleph* would be *алп* [alp], signifying *a hero* (the first among all) and *a giant* (the biggest among all), ones who are "higher" than others.

The phoneme [i], as discussed around the contrasting pair of Kyrgyz *u* vs. *uu*, provides connotations of *invisibility* (because of being *inside*). It is also evident in the word *uч* [ich], which means *inside/ within*, or *nothing* as a permanent quality (invisible because of being *inside*), and *(to) drink* (as a swift/ resolute action of putting something *inside*).

Considered as a part of "two-phoned compound word," the phoneme [u], as seen in the compound verb *ку* [qu] (to) *land* (where [k] is for *place*), likely connotes the action of *'hovering/ flying/ being lifted up before landing,'* implying that *landing* is an action that requires the object to be in a *hovering/ flying / lifted up* state first.

This is supported by another two-phoned verb, *ук* [uk], which means *(to) hear* or *listen*. Here, the notion is that hearing involves the act of sound to *get lifted/hover/ fly* first and then *land*. Such interpretation gains further support from the fact that its counterpart with the same morphemes in reverse sequence, ку, serves as the root stem for the term кулак [qulaq] (*ear*). This conveys the idea of 'a *place* [k] + that receives *hovering* [u] matter (sound) + that *sticks* [l]' (further suffix [-ak] reflects that the word is a noun).

Indeed, the abundance of two-phoned words in the Kyrgyz language is a valuable source to discern the connotations associated with individual sound in the ur-vocabulary of humanity's proto-language. When the meaning of one phoneme in such compound terms is evident, we can group them into phonological minimal sets, which makes the deducing the meaning of another root phoneme more reliable.

Consider the following set of "closed compound words" that share "stem" к—*land, place/ vicinity*: ак [aq] '*white (most visible/pure* in vicinity)' 'or '(to) *flow* from *most high up* to here '+ ук [uk] '*hear* (as a process of receiving landing of the *hovering* in vicinity sound' + ок [ɒq] '*bullet (*that flies *away over* the land*)*' + өк [œk] '*sigh of regret '(*to bust *rise* of energy/ mood) + эк [ek] '*sow (*as an act of initiating *existence* by putting seeds in the ground/ land*)*' + ык [ɯq] *snug* or *propitious* [87] *(*as a characteristic of being favorably close, which can signify a very small gap or *intimate* proximity to a warm, powerful, lucky body/matter*).*'

Correspondingly, the other then [q/k] morphemes in these words convey following meanings: [a] suggests the *most visible/ highest up* (confirming what was found before), [u] implies (to) *hover/ fly/ to be lifted up* (also seen above), [ɒ] *away* and *over*, [œ] signifies *prompt rise* (the notion which can be similarly supported by the meaning of the term бөк [bœk], the *steep hill*), [e] implies (to) *be/*

existing, and [ɯ] conveys the idea the *intimate proximity* to something of strong qualities, thus also representing opposite qualities such as of being *week, tiny or soft*.

This analysis demonstrates how phonemes in the Kyrgyz language are associated with specific connotations, allowing for a deeper understanding of word meanings and formation.

Another set of two-phoneme words helps to determine the proto-connotation of the sound [y]. While tiredness exclamation *уф* [yt] represents *narrowest* gap formed by the lips, *ym* [yt] denotes an '*extremely narrow tract* within anatomical organs, such as the breast or other,' and *yp* [yr] means (to) *bark* and *ун* [yn] the *voice*, both representing sounds produced by the mouth–a *narrow* vent of the body. The combine understanding provides a connotation of the *narrowness* for the morpheme [y]. This conclusion is also consistent with the phonetic "physiology" of producing the sound [y].

Building on the aforementioned method and leveraging the intrinsic linguistic characteristic of prolonged vowels to unveil their reverse meanings, we can endeavor to unveil the implications concealed within the prolonged counterparts of vowel morphemes, even those that are not preserved in Kyrgyz language.

Given the established connotation of the morpheme [a], it becomes plausible that its prolonged derivative [ä] may encapsulate a sense of opposition to *'being higher'* or a state of *'being lower.'* This interpretation finds additional support in the Kyrgyz term *aap* [ä], denoting the notion of being *'pressed down into the surface'* lines associated with ornaments, hand lines, or fine lines of the face.

As [y] connotes *narrowness*, its "antonym" [ÿ] has to signify the *broadness*. This is confirmed by *кyy* [kÿ], meaning 'a *melody* from the string instrument (as a spread of sound from vibration of strings.' It seems to to hint at the *broadness*, a property of the melody's spreading sound.

As [u] signifies *flying/hovering*, the meaning of its prolonged version *yy* [ü] *'poison/ poisonous* '(that makes one to "*fall down*") looks to confirm the "to be an opposite" meaning.

In a similar vein, reversing the connotations we've associated with the morphemes [œ] and [ɯ] leads us to intriguing insights.

The inverse meaning of [œ], which signifies *a prompt rise*, could imply *'a slow exhaustion or reduction,'* a concept well-illustrated by the Kyrgyz word *өзө* [œ:gœ:] (where the sound [g] is considered as a "bridge" in vowel's prolonged version), referring to *a rasp* or the action *of rasping*, suggesting a gradual reduction.

Conversely, [ɯ]'s antonym could suggest the opposite of intimate distance and the soft qualities, symbolizing *'touching tightly'* and *rough, hard* qualities, a notion supported by the Kyrgyz verb *ызы* [ɯgɯ], meaning (to) *press down*.

In our exploration of the origins of human language, we stand on the verge of an ancient linguistic realm, a proto-language, shared by our earliest ancestors. Within this realm, our forebears communicated through a rudimentary yet profoundly meaningful vocabulary. At this initial stage of proto-language development, the lexicon was far from the intricate words and phrases we know today. Instead, it was crafted from terms consisting of just a single vowel, each carrying a profound and fundamental connotation.

Based on finding from above, we can suggest that the "vowels only" stage in the Sapiens' vocabulary consisted of following terms:
- The sound [a] signified *alpha quality, being on top/well-visible*,

- while its prolonged version [ä] conveyed the opposite, *opacity and being lower*.

- Morpheme [ɒ] represented being *away/over/ above in the air* and the *realm of afterlife*.

- Correspondingly, its prolonged counterpart [ɒ:] implied the *lower in/ down below* and it can be also suggested that it use to denote the *realm of this life, the realm of mortals*.

- [u] evoked the sensation of *hovering/ flying* or *lifting up*, with

- [ü] suggesting *descent/ fall*.

- [i] embodied the concept of *within, all-encompassing*, or *invisible*, and

- [ï] denoted confirmation of *clarity*.

- [œ] indicated a *swift rise*,

- [œ:] represented *slow exhaustion/ reduction*.

- [e] conveyed *existence*, and

- [ë] implied *authority over existence*.

- [y] signaled *narrowness/ being compact*, while
- [ÿ] suggested *being spread/ vastness*.
- Meanwhile, [ɯ] encapsulated *intimate surrounding/ proximity*, and the *weak* qualities;
- [ɯː] represents action of *pressure* and *roughness*.

These single-vowel terms hypothetically constituted the very building blocks of communication for our common forefathers, representing a primal verbal proto-language. They serve as a testament to the remarkable origins of human expression and understanding, providing valuable insights into the fundamental concepts that shaped our earliest means of communication.

Single Consonants

A clear comprehension of the connotations of primordial single-phoneme vowel morphemes (from the previous section), along with the abundance of two-phoneme, vowel-consonant terms in Kyrgyz language, offers us an opportunity to discern the meanings behind consonant "proto-morphemes" as well.

For example, *aŭ* [aj], signifying a (new) moon, implies an object that is *first visible* (for [a]) in the night sky with two tapering ends that bend towards the inside. When the known meaning of the phoneme [a] is left aside, the remaining part of the meaning will shed light on the connotation associated with the phoneme [j] as representing *(bending) protruding ends*. This interpretation is further supported by the verb *uŭ* [ij], meaning *(to) bend*, to be interpreted as an act of 'directing *ends/edges* [j] +

towards *inside* [i]. Interestingly, the notion of *being* inside related to the phone [i] is also clearly visible within the English preposition *in* and its derivatives.

Similarly, from the diverse meanings of Kyrgyz word *am* [at], (such as to *shoot*, *name* and *horse*), we can decode connotations that are signified by the phoneme [t]. Knowing that [a] conveys the sense of *first* (before me), *elevated*, *visible* or *identifiable*, we can suggest that other "morpheme" [t] represents various *entities* or *matters*, such as:

- *Bodies* or *structure*: As in case of *horse* ('a *body* that elevates me')

- *Thing*: As in case of *shooting* ('making *things* to be *up*')

- *Matters:* As in case of *name* ('a *matter* that makes me *up/* identifiable among others').

The word *ama* [ata] for *father*, a possible derivative of *am* with the meaning *name*, reflects the Kyrgyz tradition of paternal naming rights. This suggests that *ama* can be interpreted as '*one* who came *before* me and gave me my *name*.' Interestingly, *ata* ata' is also found in many Indo-European languages (See Volume I).

As we know, the morpheme [e] carries the connotation *existence*. The "meaning" of the morpheme [ʃ] emerges from the term эш [eʃ] for *partner* or *comrade*—someone who accompanies another, making them "more then one," thus conveying the idea of *togetherness* and *multitude* in general.

While above [ʃ] represents the idea of *multitude* in general sense, the [b/v/p/f]—which are interchangeable in Kyrgyz—appear to signify a sense of "selves" multitude. This is exemplified by the word биз [biz] (meaning *us*), which can be analyzed as 'multitude [b] + within [i], which is either stable or subject to reduction [z] (a concept to be elaborated further).

Another two-phoned term with one of the morphemes signifying existence ([e]) would be эн [en]. Meaning size/width or mark/tag of or on the object it can be understood as conveying idea of 'a thing that represent existence [e] of + a particular object [n].' Thus, the logic for second morpheme[n] is that it connotes a concept of an object.

Moreover, the term uч [iʨ], previously discussed and conveying the concept of being internal or (to) drink, implies that the phoneme [ʨ] represents a permanent quality or resolute action. This interpretation aligns with the meanings of other words, such as ач [aʨ], signifying hunger (a state when one feels like their belly is open) and (to) open (a quick, resolute action), as well as уч [uʨ], symbolizing a tip (a permanently 'hovering in the air' part of an object) and (to) fly (a resolute action).

As the above case illustrates, comparing several two-phoned terms from the Kyrgyz language that share the same consonant is another way to identify the meaning of that consonant as a morpheme. If we consider a set of words containing the phoneme [ʤ/ʥ], we find аж [aʤ]—an onomatopoeia for a barking shout (a sound that spreads far away); жаа [ʥä], meaning arrow or precipitation process (both covering large distances); and жуу [ʥü], meaning to wash out (removing dirt—a substance associated with the ground/Earth). From these examples, we can infer that the connotation of [ʤ/ʥ] is related to the concept of the Earth surface, implying a large scale or far-reaching presence, similar to but broader than the morpheme [k] (which denotes place or vicinity). This is further supported by the Kyrgyz term for *Earth—Жер* [ʤer], which potentially signifies '*Earth* [ʤ] + *existence* [e] + *cover* [r] (as will be elaborated next).'

Larger sets of phonological data can be employed to further refine the meanings our progenitors attributed to single-phone terms or morphemes.

Here's the next phonological minimal set that corroborates the meaning identified for the phoneme [r]:

- *ap* [ar], with [a] standing for *best visibility*: *'far away'* (view *covering* Earth's surface, a horizon), *'dissimilar'* (with different *cover/coating*) and *'(to) tire or wear out'* (as a gradual process of *covering* distance to the *horizon* between life and afterlife).

- *up* [ir], with [i] symbolizing *inner*: *'before all '*(being one who *took over* the inner group), *'all within'* (*covering* all together).

- *yp* [ur], with [u] for the *hovering/ flying*: *'gnarl'* (hovering *cover/ coating*) or *'(to) hit/ build'* (the process of lifting up and laying down *a cover/ coating*).

- *op* [ɒr], with [ɒ] for *above/away/in the air*: *'pit'* (a place where the *cover* went away/above/into the air) and *'(to) mow'* (process of throwing away the *coating* of Earth).

- *өp* [œr], with [œ] standing for *prompt move*: *'ascent'* (*surface* that *promptly rises*) or *'(to) weave'* (*taking over* the threads).

- *эp* [er], with [e] for *existence*: *'hero'* or *'noble'* (one who *takes over* the matters or *covers* responsibilities to assure wellbeing of others).

- *ыp* [ɯr], with [ɯ] for *close-by surrounding* and *weakness*:

'*song*' (soft sound that *covers* the surrounding).

The findings discussed above provide compelling evidence to associate the morpheme [r] with the connotation of *coating/cover/protection* that *spreads all over*. Interestingly, with this understanding, we can interpret previously discussed *yp* ([yr], *to bark*), as a more directed ([y] representing *narrow*) sound covering ([r]) the area. Similarly, *ыp* [ɯr], meaning *a song*, as a broader sound that *covers* [r] + *intimate surrounding* [ɯ] (perhaps initially referring to lullabies).'

Curiously, the English word *surrounding* (as derivative of *round*) also demonstrates a link to the primordial meaning revealed for the morpheme [r].

The shorter version of the phonological minimal sets— *the phonological minimal pairs* in the Kyrgyz language, in turn, can help us to better understand the connotations of interchangeably used phonemes such as the case with suffixes -*c* [s] and -*з* [z].

Let's consider some minimal pairs:

1. *ac* [as] '(*to*) *hang* up 'vs. *аз* [az] '*to be/ becoming small/ smaller*'

 - Interpretation: with [a] symbolizing visibility, *ac* conveys the idea of action to *make* an *exterior* of the object *more* visible; while *аз* implies *reduction* of the object's *exterior* or *its visibility*.

2. *ыc* [ɯs] '*exuding* aroma 'vs. *ыз* [ɯz] imitation of *persisting and* intimately close *irritating* noise (by mosquito, bee...);

 - Interpretation: *ыc,* where [ɯ] refers to proximity, conveys the connotation of object's *exterior* smell *getting stronger* with increased proximity. On the other hand, *ыз* brings the message of *enduring* and *destructive* quality of the sound within a short distance to the *exterior* of the object.

3. Another pair with explained above phoneme [ɯ], but now also supported by initiating phoneme [q], which symbolizes the *place*: кыс [qɯs] '*to press*' vs. кыз [qɯz] '*a daughter*' or '*girl (in general)*'
 - Interpretation: кыс carries the connotation of '*continuous* and *increasing* in force pressure applied on the object's *exterior*. 'The first two letters of the term denoting '*intimate proximity* to the *ground*, 'it has to be seen as '*making* an object close to the *ground*. 'In contrast, кыз signifies someone towards whom pressure and force *always* has *to be restricted*.

4. өс [œs] '*(to) grow/ develop* 'vs. өз [œz] '*of self*'
 - Interpretation: with [œ] implying a *rise* in quality, өс suggests an action of *making exterior* of yourself *continuously* rising, while өз implies a *lasting absence* in rise of one-self's exterior—a state of being self, as it is.

From these examples, we deduce that both suffixes -*c* and -*з* convey a *lasting exterior* quality related to the stem's meaning or, in case of verbs, *continuous action* towards the object's *exterior*. While -*c* is used to signify *growth* or *an increase in* that quality or action, conversely, when -*з* is employed, it implies either *lasting absence of change* or *action—constraint*. This understanding underscores the dual nature of both suffixes and how they can be interchangeably used. They not only convey the infinite nature of the terms they help construct but also introduce nuanced variation in the state or process described by the term.

As the place of the morpheme in two-phoned

rudimentary words shouldn't change much the meaning that it implies, we can also test the above interpretations with terms that have sounds [s] and [z] at the beginning of such terms. For example, the archaic verb сы [sɯ] '(to) dismount (by hitting)' can be understood as 'continuously keep intimate distance to object's *exterior* till it breaks.' Similarly, the imitative word for sound зың [zɯɴ] may denote a similar but restrained notion of '*persisting* sound from the object's *exterior*, which doesn't break when hit (as a notion of intimate distance).' In both cases, the general connotations provided by the considered phones match what was determined from the earlier analysis.

The stage in the development of the ur-vocabulary discussed above marked a significant expansion in the foundation for new words. In addition to the terms consisting of single vowel or click sound, this stage introduced the possibility of creating words with both vowel-consonant and consonant-vowel combinations. These could be grouped into pairs based on the shared vowel and consonant.

While these rudimentary words may not have greatly differed in their overarching connotations, having a range of options allowed our proto ancestors for the first time the ability to refine meaning and produce more precise terms. This development undoubtedly advanced the expressive capabilities of our early proto-ancestors.

For instance, let's revisit the word *ap* [ar], which in Kyrgyz holds a complex philosophical meaning signifying *faraway/ horizon, various* and *getting wearied* [73]. Intriguingly, its reverse combination of [ar] — [ra] was employed by the ancient Egyptians as the name for one of their gods, sun god *Ra*, the name that now can be understood as 'one that *covers all* to *horizon*.'

As encountered previously with the phoneme [q/k/g] denoting *place*, it's worth noting that standalone single consonants can also carry specific meanings. While consonants are not typically pronounced individually, it's possible that these phonemes had specific two-phoned forms to represent their core meanings. It's akin to how the letter *к* [q] is pronounced as [qɯ] in today's Kyrgyz alphabet or how the English letter *b* is pronounced as [bi].

This is also evident from the phonological patterns in the Kyrgyz language of consonants like *л* [l] and *р* [r] tending to be pronounced with an initial vowel [ɯ] (or [i]) when borrowed from other languages. For example borrowed from Russian term for the electric bubble *лампочка* [lampoʨka] will pronounced in Kyrgyz as [ɯlampoʨka] and word for frame *рама* [rama] pronounced [ɯrama]. Thus, it is plausible to consider that as separate one-phoned terms *л* and *р* might sounded as [(ɯ)l] and [(ɯ)r]. This notion is further supported by the existence of these words (*ыл* and *ыр*) and numerous phonological derivatives in modern Kyrgyz vocabulary that begin with these phonemes.

Given their potential antiquity, the Kyrgyz sounds *л/ыл* and *р/ыр* may be among the earliest elements of protohuman vocabulary. Within this context, their meanings (*ыл* - *a cataract/surfer's eye* and *ыр* - *a song*) can be interpreted as 'a matter that *landed* on the eye' and 'the sound that *covers all around.*'

Examples of the "stem morpheme" [l] in Kyrgyz *ылдый* [ɯldɯj] (*downwards*) and *ылдыра* [ɯldɯra] (*being exhausted*), hints at a *downwards movement* and the connotation of "*sticking down.*"

Another consonant that naturally produced with the aid of the sound is [ɴ], pronounced as [ɯɴ]. Its meaning can be inferred from the same Kyrgyz word ың, particularly as notable in the expression 'ың(-жың) жок' [ɯɴ(-d͡ʒɯɴ) d͡ʒoq], signifying *tranquility* and literally translating to 'no ың at all,' where ың represent disturbance. By interpreting the morpheme [ɯ] in [ɯɴ]—which denotes *disturbance*—as indicating *intimate proximity*, we can deduce that [ɴ] evokes sense of something *sadden* or emotionally *immediate*. This interpretation is supported by the onomatopoeic expressions such as ыңк [ɯɴq], which suggests a sudden event, and ыңаа [ɯɴä], used to describe an infant's cry.

Based on the research of this book, the single-consonant based terms of hypothetical ur-vocabulary can be summarized as follows: [b/v/p/ɸ]: This group, represented by Kyrgyz б, is associated with the concept of *us and plurality*. [m]: corresponds to the idea of *self* and *singularity*. [j]: Represents the notion of *ends/ protruding edges*. [g/k/q/h/ɣ/χ/ʁ]: Similar to the Kyrgyz к, these phones symbolize *place, dirt*, or *location*. [l]: *attachment to/ (co-) location/ adhesion*. [d/t]: Corresponding to the often interchangeable Kyrgyz д and m, these phones denote *structure or body*. [d͡ʒ/d͡z]: Relates to *Earth/ground* or *earthly matters*. [z]: Like the Kyrgyz з, signifies *continuity or restriction of the quality or action*. [n]: Represents *object(s)*. [ɴ]: speaks about *immediacy*. [r]: Relates to *a coating/cover/protection* or *taking over*. [s]: Signifies *making continuous rise* or *an increase* in quality and exterior. [t͡ɕ]: Denotes a *resolute action*. [ʂ/ʃ]: Based on Kyrgyz ш, provides connotations of *joint* or *cumulative* quality.

As mentioned earlier, within the primordial list of consonants, we also find the click sounds. Two of these, [kʼ] used to imitate soothing animal sounds and [ǂ] used to express disappointment, have enduring usage in the

Kyrgyz language and can be added to the rudimentary vocabulary of our common ancestors.

Combines Vocabulary

Indeed, the above single-consonant morphemes, combined with the single-vowel and prolonged-vowels ones and click sounds, would have collectively formed the foundational elements of early human communication. In their rudimentary but profoundly meaningful form, they conveyed fundamental concepts essential for survival and understanding in the nascent stages of human language.

In the ancient realm of human proto-language, where our distant ancestors first ventured into the world of communication, a rudimentary yet profoundly meaningful vocabulary took shape. This vocabulary was unlike the intricate words and phrases of modern languages; instead, it was crafted from single vowel and single consonant terms. Each of these simple morphemes carried profound and fundamental connotations. It serves as a window into the remarkable origins of human expression, offering insights into the very roots of our ability to convey complex ideas and emotions through language. It represents the embodiment of our shared, ancestral consciousness and the foundational building blocks upon which the rich tapestry of human languages has been woven over millennia.

Putting together all previously discussed single sound unit terms, we can form the assumed vocabulary of the basic initial morphemes in the humanities—the building blocks of any further developed language:

1. [a] (corresponding to Kyrgyz **A**) - The visible/high/best/alpha/available/apart.

2. [ä] (**Аа**) - To lower down/ below the level.

3. [b/v/p/ɸ] (**Б**) - Concept of 'us 'and plurality.

4. [d/t] (**Д**) - Entity/body/structure/matter.

5. [e] (**Э/Е**) - To be or existing.

6. [ë] (**Э:/Е:**) - Owner/ to be in control of someone/ something.

7. [ʤ/ʥ] (**Ж**) - Earth/ ground/ land.

8. [z] (**З**) - Continuation or restriction of the quality or action.

9. [i] (**И**) - Within, all-encompassing or inclusive.

10. [ï] (**И:**) - Confirmation/ clarity.

11. [j] (**Й**) - Protruding/ protuberance, a notion of edges/ tapering ends and being extra or in abundance.

12. [g/k/q/h] (**К**) - Place/ vicinity, (to) land.

13. [l] (**Л**) - Attachment to/ (co-) location.

14. [m] (**М**) - Concept of self and singularity.

15. [n] (**Н**) - Concept of the particular object.

16. [ɴ] (**Ң**) - Concept of Sudden event or Immediacy.

17. [ɒ] (**О**) - Being above/out there, over/ in the air. Also signifies the afterlife realm.

18. [ɒ:] (**О:**) - Being on the other side, down there. Also signifies the real realm.

19. [œ] (**Ө**) - Prompt action or quick rise/increase.

20. [œ:] (**Ө:**) - Slow action or gradual exhausting or decreasing.

21. [r] (**Р**) - Coating, fully/all covering.

22. [s] (**С**) - The exterior and continuous rise/ increase in quality.

23. [u] (**У**) - Hovering/ flying or the process of lifting up.

24. [ü] (**У:**) - Following down.

25. [ɣ] (**Ү**) - Notion of narrowness, being compact.

26. [ÿ] (**Ү:**) - Notion of broadness, being spread out.

27. [tɕ] (**Ч**) - Resolute action, permanent quality.

28. [ʂ/ʃ] (**Ш/ Щ**) - Joint/cumulative/compound quality, togetherness.

29. [ɯ] (**Ы**) - Close proximity/surroundings and the weak/soft qualities.

30. [ɯː] (**Ы:**) - Pressure and toughness.

31. ** [ɬ] ** - Expression of disappointment and disagreement.

32. **[k']** - An onomatopoeia of "friendly talk" to an animal.

These single phoned "terms" formed the foundation of early human communication, conveying fundamental concepts essential for survival and understanding in their primal form. This primal ur-vocabulary represents the remarkable origins of human expression and the roots of our ability to convey complex ideas and emotions through language, reflecting our common root consciousness itself.

FURTHER EVOLUTION

All together, connections reviewed above underscore the intricate interplay between single sound units and relevant meanings, not only within Kyrgyz but also across languages, providing valuable insights into the shared origins of linguistic expressions and their cultural contexts.

The "dictionary of the first 32 words" can be instrumental in decoding the rudimentary terms of our ur-ancestors'language from the distant past. To demonstrate how, let's take some imitative words from the proto-human vocabulary discussed before.

Caption of the Chapter Opening Image (Fig. 3): Kyrgyz yurt, A Nomadic Home. (Source: Public Domain. See List of Figures)

The image showcases a Kyrgyz yurt, a portable dwelling renowned for its ease of assembly and disassembly. In Kyrgyz, these tents are generically referred to as *боз yŭ*—the '*gray house*', a term that by its reference to a house underscores their historical significance as one of humanity's earliest housing innovations. The use of the word "house" in the Kyrgyz term emphasizes the yurt's role as a fundamental dwelling.

One of them, *AJA [adʒa] 'mother, older female relative' ('senior person" in Kyrgyz), can now be analyzed as a compound word composed of three "stems" from the ur-vocabulary. It can be interpreted as 'the first one [a] + who has the right to raise (her) voice so loudly that it "takes over" [a] + entire Earth/ground [dʒ].'

Another word, *BUR [bur] 'ashes, dust,' can be understood as 'a multitude [b] + hovering [u] + and covering all [r].'

Enhanced Connotations

The gradual transformation in the meaning, with no change in the form of primordial terms, is also notable when examining two-phoned words from the Kyrgyz language. These words, originating from very ancient times, unveil unwritten stories of prehistory.

Take the word *yŭ* [yj], which, as a verb, denotes (to) *stock* or (to) *pile*, and as a noun, a *house*. It takes us back to the times of very early sapiens, the cave people, and hints at their natural habitat being mountainous areas where caves are abundant. This insight provides an understanding that long-distance migration at that time would have been only possible along the foothills, leading to the emergence of IAMC (Inner Asian Mountains Corridor) and further development with the invention of movable huts.

Of the two meanings of the term, the verb, understood as '(to) *collect in one place*,' logically appeared before its counterpart noun. Thus, people would call their house the place where they stowed their belongings, the station, the base, or the storage house. Initially, it might have been a cave, and when they moved to another place, it would be another cave and so forth. Gradually, with "technological" development, the time came to invent movable huts. The progenitors continued to call them that way (as *боз уй* [boz yj] – the yurt (Fig. 3 above), and Kyrgyz still continue to call their stationary houses *уй*.

Here is also an example of even more sophisticated evolution. While the word *ой* [oj], encountered earlier, signifies both (to) excavate and, in a further evolved meaning, *thought*, and the term for the *pit* (*аң* [aṅ]) also translates to a more sophisticated term, *intellect*, intriguing parallels can be drawn. The increase in the properties of the first term (*ой*), representing extended excavation, eventually leads to the emergence of a pit (*аң*). Similarly, the union of *ой* (the thoughts) again culminates in the formation of *аң* (intellect). Viewed cumulatively, it is evident that the progenitors saw intellect as a result of deep, thoughtful contemplation—an intellectually profound consideration!

Moreover, we recognize that the richness and duality of meaning are among the most fascinating attributes of these early, embryonic terms. Such characteristics can be attributed to the entire stage of orality in prehistoric times and must be carefully considered when attempting to understand terms and texts from early languages—including Sanskrit in the context of early yoga. These languages, rooted in primary orality, inherently lack the precision and practicality seen in later written forms.

Reduplication

The subsequent logical phase in the progression of proto-human language development (after two, three phoned terms became a norm) would likely involve the reduplication of those simple stem words, akin to the prolonged vowels that evolved once early sapiens mastered short ones.

This assumption is also supported by the fact that reduplication, which resembles *babbling*, is a natural part of the language acquisition process for infants. Such archaic linguistic feature of reduplication is particularly prominent in the Kyrgyz language, as previously discussed in its resemblance to ancient Ubaid/Sumerian (See Volume I).

Kyrgyz exhibits various forms of reduplication, including *full reduplication, initial* and *final partial reduplication* with changes in the base, *reduplication of consonant, triplication*, which can actually be re-multiplied any number of times, making this feature most closely resembles babbling. In essence, this technique of word formation represents an elemental way to enrich the meaning of the stem.

The presence of numerous forms of such embryonic word formation options in Kyrgyz language becomes evident through examples like the fundamental two-phoneme term *ак* [aq], which we have already explored in depth.

Ак signifies *white* and *(to) flow*, with the connotation of *pure* water coming from the *'openly visible in the first place, high up glaciers above the horizon* [a] + down to our *place* [k].' However, when fully reduplicated as *акак* [aqaq], the meaning shifts to *precious*, conveying the notion of utmost purity or preciousness.

Furthermore, in other forms of reduplication the ending segment of the base changes to [p] or its double in initial reduplicants. So other terms derived from *ак* [aq] are: *ап-ак* [ap-aq] and its variant *аппак* [appaq] translate to *very white*; *ананак* [apapaq] signifying *absolutely white*. The "any number of times re-multiplication," in the case of *ак* often extended by diminutive suffix [-aj], sounds like *анананана...акай* [apapapapap...aqaj], similar to how in English one might say *very-very-very...very white*.

This linguistic phenomenon is not only fascinating in its own right but also offers valuable insights into the way ancient languages evolved and how early humans communicated and assigned meaning to their surroundings. Once again, we can see that the Kyrgyz language, with its rich linguistic heritage, serves as a window into the early stages of human language development and word formation.

Agglutinative Development

Being an agglutinative language, Kyrgyz practically demonstrates how the proto-human vocabulary evolved further. Here is an example of a possible evolutionary path within one morphological chain, leading from a very materially-minded term to a term associated with the cosmos.

As discussed earlier, the first arose vowel sounds, including **ы* [ɯ], signifying *intimate distance*. When speech organs developed the ability to pronounce consonants, the utterance **ж* [dʒ] denoting *ground* appeared. With improved ability to mimic richer sounds, the onomatopoeia for the sound produced by flying or moving around insects, *ыж* [ɯdʒ], emerged, categorizing insects as creatures 'intimately close to the ground' to differentiate them from also flying birds. Given the flexibility of order in the pronunciation of just two units, its reverse form [dʒɯ] joined in with the same connotation.

Further assisted by the morpheme *л [l] for (to) *stick/ be attached*, it brought to life the still-existing compound word *жыл* [ʤɯl], conveying the notion of an action of changing place while being 'constantly *attached* [l] + *close* [ɯ] + to the *ground* [ʤ],' denoting the verb (to) *move*. It likely originated as a request to move to the next person when everyone sat together on the ground.

Gradually, as the need arose to discuss the annual events of nature, the term *жыл* began to indicate the year as a '*move of time since the same scenery of the past.*' The reminiscent words, *avail* and *ril* were also used in Etruscan, the pre-Latin language.

With the word for (to) *move* in place, derivatives with related meanings started to emerge. First came terms for objects in nature from an intimate distance, such as a fast-*moving* horse, *жылкы* [ʤɯl-qɯ] or graciously *moving* snake, *жалаан* [ʤɯl-än], the word of significant value in early beliefs—Hittite myth about the serpent *Illuyanka* (Refer to Volume I).

The form of the stem verb further developed to describe a third party moving as *жылды* [ʤɯl-dɯ]. With the use of the suffix -з [z] denoting the absence of the action, the idea emerged to call a distant, motionless object in the sky *жылдыз* [ʤɯl-dɯ-z], signifying stars.

Decoding A Deeper Meaning

Based on Kyrgyz language we can also find very interesting and difficult to predict possible twists in the logic of human vocabulary development, which "connects the dots" between terms that morphologically are distanced even further apart.

Take a very basic word, in its appearance: *cow, уй* [uj]. Its "stems" gives us the connotation of an animal with *'lifted up/hovering* ([u]) + *protuberances* [j]. 'This further takes us to its 'derivative 'word a nest—*уя* [uja], as by deciphering it provides a notion of the structure that has *'lifted up* [u] + *protuberances* [j] + situated *high up* ([a]).'

With the essential ingredients for advanced word formation in place, our common ancestors began to assemble an even greater variety of terms with more nuanced, specific, and applied meanings. As discussed in Volume I, scholars have identified 27 such terms. Let's explore some additional possibilities.

Consider the shortest possible Kyrgyz verb э [e], which signifies the *existence* itself. This verb is not only a notable root in many Kyrgyz words but also shares linguistic connection with the ancient Latin word for existence, *essentia,* or even the Proto-Indo-European root **es* for *to be* [33]. This connection is further reflected in the Kyrgyz philosophical term эс [es] for *mind/consciousness,* a topic we will explore in more detail in the relevant chapter.

The primeval exclamation *oŭ* [oj] discussed earlier, is also present in the Russian language. Its additional connotations of to *hollow out* and a *cavity in the ground* intriguingly correspond with meaning of the English *void* that contains this morpheme. It roots back to Latin, ultimately stemming from PIE **eue*, signifying *to leave, abandon* or *give out* [31]. Considering its additional meaning discussed above, t*h*ought, we can infer that to our ancestors, thoughts were perceived akin to the act of *'emptying the mind from the ideas.'*

The Russian/Slavic word for the *joker,* on the origin of which there is no common view among the scholars, is pronounced and written precisely the same way as Kyrgyz word from folklore *шут* [ṣut], denoting a *jokester* character. If we are to decipher it, the meaning would be *'lifting up* [u] + *shared* [ṣ] + *object/matter* (mood) [t].

Another Russian word, *жижа* [ʐɯʐa], meaning *liquid mad,* shares a linguistic similarity with Kyrgyz *жижи* [ʤiʤi] for the *liquid manure*. Both words seem to be related to the stem *жи* [ʤi], which can be decoded as droppings 'from *inside* [i] + on the *ground* [ʤ/ʐ].' The stem *жи* [ʤi] also gives rise to close in meaning term like *жин* [ʤin], discussed in Volume I. In Kyrgyz it denotes the intestinal liquid considered to have properties of bile (transparent and bitter in taste). Same word is also found in English (gin) for a type of strong alcohol and Arabic (jinn) for the bitter and invisible (as transparent or "liquid") creature.

The construction of another Kyrgyz term, *сан* [san], which shows linguistic connection to the yogic term Sankhya (as discussed in the preceding volume), strongly aligns with its fundamental essence. Its meanings— *number/count, a body part,* or *thigh*—correspond well with its construction as [s] (exterior) + [a] (well visible) + [n] object(s)].

Delving deeper into the root of this word we see *са* [sa], which deciphers as 'one whose *exterior/view* [s] is *well seen/visible* [a]' and means *you* in Kyrgyz. Its "derivative," *сар* [sar], translates to *gold,* and can be deciphered as 'whose *view* [s] + is *seen* [a] + as *all covering* or *dominating.*' Interestingly, in Hebrew, a similar word denotes *chief/ ruler/prince* [18], reflecting a similar quality.

Even more intriguing, this morpheme appears in Kyrgyz adjective *кайсар* [kajsar] (where the *кай* [kaj] root denotes *noble* [19]), which describes *resolute, brave and strong* person—a fitting description for an emperor, as seen in the name of the Roman Julius *Caesar* (1-st AD dictator), pronounced exactly as [kaẹ.sar]. His cognomen (a "nickname"), *Caesar*, said to be of unknown origin, became an Imperial title in many languages including Ancient Greek (*Kaîsar*), German (*Kaiser*) and Russian (*Tsar*) [17].

As discussed in the first volume, the further evolved word *capa* [sara] translates to *the best selected*, and is found in the Sanskrit name of Goddess *Sarasvati*, with a closely related meaning. While similar connotation is also reflected in the etymology of the name *Sarah*, of Hebrew origin, meaning *princess* [18]—a connection that can also be seen in the Kyrgyz word for *a palace*, *сарай* [saraj], often preceded by *ак (white)* discussed above.

In the framework of "primeval linguistics" prolonging a "root word" like *ca* must logically produce a word with the reverse meaning to it. This would imply a word that connotes 'an *exterior* [s] that is *NOT well visible* [ä].' Kyrgyz word *саа* [sä], which translates to as *to milk* (or collect food into a receptacle such as *milk to bucket)*, serves as 'make an *exterior* [s] of an object to be *not visible* [ä].'

Intriguingly, the Kyrgyz term *Кут*, a word of philosophical significance, closely resembles the English word *good*. As explored in Volume I, it encompasses a range of meanings, including *happiness, luck, abundance, or prosperity* [25]. Ultimately, it signifies all possible forms of Goodness in our lives. The term can be understood as a combination of the "stems" [k] (signifying one's *place*) + [u] (for *descending* or *flying* down) and [t] (for the *entity*), conveying the connotation of '*entity that descends upon us.*' This suggests that the divine was always envisioned as coming from above.

Related English word of Proto-Germanic origin, *God*,

based on its corresponding one-morpheme structure, is evidently rooted deep in the primordial vocabulary as well. Although its Proto-Germanic root *gudą is considered of uncertain origin, a similar word *Куда* [quda] persists in the Kyrgyz language. It unquestionably traces back to the stem *Кут*, which in addition to its above meaning, also represents divine and cosmic matters. This term has its origins in an even earlier onomatopoeia *ку* [qu], which, resembling a call from the "bird's vocabulary," is used to land the prey bird.

Additionally, one of the Kyrgyz words for God, *Кудай* [qudaj], while marked as of Iranian origin in Yudahin's dictionary, is clearly rooted in the above Kyrgyz term *Кут*. This places its stem in the pre-Proto-Indo-Iranian linguistic category, reinforcing the findings of the *Kyrgyz And Pre-Proto-Indo-European* (PIE) *Links* chapter of Volume I.

The term *Обо* [ovd] signifies *heaven/ air space*. Its construction consists of two phonemes *o* [ɒ] and *б* [v/b]. As shown earlier, in the Kyrgyz stem root *o* provides the connotation of *over/away in the air* and *б* of *us/plurality*, which together denotes '*arial matter* [ɒ] + *in plentitude* [b]' or 'matter *over* ([ɒ]) + *us* ([b]).'

These phonemes can also be observed in PIE languages through English words like *Over, O'er, On, tOp* for [ɒ] and *We, Both (of us), Between (us)* for [v/b]. As part of the Kyrgyz compound word *Обо-эне* [ovd-ene], which translates as *Fore-mother* (The Mother that *was before* and is *over* us), *обо* gives meaning close to English *fore- (us)* [21]. Notably, this Kyrgyz term resonates with counterparts in other ancient languages, such as PIE *upo*, Latin *sub*, Ancient Greek *hupo*, and Sanskrit *upa* [22].

The word *yp* [ur], as previously discussed (See Volume I), means *gnarl* or *(to) hit/ build* in Kyrgyz and provides connotation of the symbol of inception (from which further growth *comes out)*. Similarly, as a prefix in English/ German rooted in PIE, it fulfills a similar role. We can decipher the meaning of [ur] as 'initially *hovering* [u] and then descending to *cover* [r].' In case of *hitting* and *building* it would denote an act and as a *gnarl*—that matter that descended/laid to *cover* the surface.

Also previously touched upon in regards to the noble hero *Эр-Төштүк*, the *'Noble Chest Armor'* (Volume I), the term *эр* [er] (*exists* [e] + to *cover* (protect, to be responsible for the family/clan–in its meaning as *a husband/nobleman*) [r]) similarly to German *herr* signifies the *nobility*.

Another linguistic connection can be found between the English word *toy*, whose origin remains uncertain but originally meant a *funny story*, and the same Kyrgyz word *той* [toj], which denotes a *celebration* or a *fun gathering*.

It's truly fascinating to observe how the Kyrgyz language reveals captivating connections with the Proto-Indo-European (PIE) group of languages through its ancient, structured root words. As discussed in Volume I, these connections provide intriguing glimpses into the earliest ties between these linguistic traditions, potentially placing Kyrgyz within the pre-PIE branch. To reinforce examples from Volume I, let's examine some instances within the context of the "first 32 words vocabulary of homo sapiens."

The Kyrgyz word for *a name* is *ам* [at], and when analyzed through the lens of "primordial vocabulary," it can be interpreted as 'a word that provides *visibility* [a] + for *body/structure* [t].'

This insightful interpretation extends to its derivative, *ama* [ata], meaning a *father*. Viewed from this perspective, *ama* can be deciphered as 'one who pronounced my *name* [at] + *first* [a], 'aligning with the Kyrgyz tradition of the father having the first right to choose a name for his child.

This term also reveals intriguing linguistic connections across different cultures and languages, sharing an identical meaning with PIE, Ancient Greek, and Latin *atta* or Hittite *attas* [25]. Beyond the Kyrgyz phrases '*ama кызы* '[ata kızı] '*father's daughter* 'or '*ama баласы* '[ata balası] '*father's son*, 'which express the idea of a child making their father proud, English phrases like *attagirl* and *attaboy* can similarly be interpreted.

As in Kyrgyz the phoneme [b] replaces [v] placed at the beginning of a word, the English term *we*, which has PIE roots as *wéy* and is akin to Sanskrit *vayám* finds a close counterpart in Kyrgyz *биз* [biz], conveying the same meaning [26].

Similarly, while the English word *me* finds its roots in PIE *me-*, Ancient Greek *eme*, Latin *me* and Sanskrit *mam* [27]. In Kyrgyz, this meaning is conveyed through *мен* [mɛn], with its form *ма* [mä] signifying *to/ for me*.

While the roots of the modern international word denoting the low-pitched spectrum of sounds, *bass*, and the English adjective *base* can be traced back to the Latin *bassus*, which denotes *stumpy* or *low* and is said to be of uncertain origin [30], the Kyrgyz verb *бас* [bas] signifies the action of *pressing* or *lowering* down, giving the object those particular qualities.

The stem *жак* [d͡ʑaq] signifies *the near side*. In its directive form *жакта* [d͡ʑaqta], it conveys the meaning of *near* (of a certain position), bearing resemblance to the English term *juxta(-position)* of Latin origin with the same meaning [29].

Similarly, the English word *shield*, although said to derive from PIE *(s)kelH- meaning to *cut/split* [28], more closely corresponds to the Kyrgyz verb *шилте* [ʃilte], denoting the movement of the arm precisely as one does when protecting themselves with a shield.

The Kyrgyz word *кап* [qap], meaning *(to) grasp* and *form/sack*, also offers an intriguing linguistic connection to English. The English *cape*, derived from Latin *cappa* (hooded cloak) of uncertain origin [34], can be considered a type of *sack* specifically intended for covering the body. Interestingly, the initial morpheme [qa] of *кап* can be decoded as *'above* [a] + *the place* [q],' suggesting a link to the concept of *covering*. Moreover, the English word *cap*, translates as *капкак* [qapqak] in Kyrgyz, which derives from the same root *кап* (in its meaning of *to grasp*). Similarly, the English word *captivity*, originating from Latin *captivitatem* and PIE *kap* (meaning *to grasp*) [35], mirrors the Kyrgyz concept of *кап*.

Kyrgyz version of the term mountain, *тоо* [tæ:], can be deciphered as 'a *structure* [t] + for the *real realm (or* with *other* side) [ɒ:].' While the concept of a high up living place corresponds to the Kyrgyz habitat, the idea of '*with other side*' is phonetically echoed in the English words *top* and *tall*. The latter can also be interpreted as the property of being of 'great height, like a mountain. 'Similarly, the German word *toll* potentially conveys a sense of something extraordinary, or 'great as a mountain.' Both of these interpretations align with a deep sense of admiration for mountains in Kyrgyz culture, which has persisted throughout the entire history of the Kyrgyz people, who have long chosen mountain ridges as their habitat.

The construction of the Kyrgyz anatomical terms, which show similarities to their Proto-Indo-European counterparts, also well align with their meanings.

In addition to previously discussed terms for the *thigh/body parts* ([san]) and *eye* ([gœz]), the Kyrgyz term *ooz* [ɒ:z], meaning *mouth* (same as its Latin counterpart, *os,* as discussed in Volume I), remarkably represents an object ensuring 'life in the *realm of mortals* [ɒ:] + that *continuously deteriorates* [z]. 'This symbolizes a fundamental truth of human life— the necessity to eat every day, which ultimately culminates in the inability to do so, marking the completion of life. This term potentially echoes from the earliest stages of meaningful communication among early Homo sapiens.

Furthermore, an intriguing linguistic nuance arises when we consider the embryonic word formation characteristic that changes connotations with a prolonged stem. By contrasting *ooz* with the word *oz* [ɒz], signifying *to spurt away*, we unveil an imagery of the mouth as an organ impeding agility. This captivating linguistic interplay reveals the power of embryonic oratory wisdom, cautioning against the hazards of excessive mouth usage, potentially associated with overeating or producing unnecessary noise.

While in the first scenario, this overindulgence directly leads to shortened life span either by generating disease or loss of agility, in the second one might result in overlooking potential danger. These linguistic insights not only offer a unique glimpse into the daily life of our distant ancestors in the wild, it also suggests a reflection of how deep and distant are the roots of self-care wisdom of what is yoga today.

Deciphering Kyrgyz word for *eye*, көз [gœz], that was related to the Ancient Greek Argos in the Volume I, reveals a meaning that can be interpreted as *'place* [g] that + *promptly moves* [œ] + *continuously but eventually stops* [z].' Interestingly, both, in sound and meaning, this term bears a resemblance to the English word *gaze*, which, although of unclear origin, is associated with the sense of vision [32].

Decoding another intriguing example of an anatomical term shared between Proto-Indo-European (PIE) and the Kyrgyz language, English word *'foot'* represented as *'бут'* [but] in Kyrgyz, we can understand it as a combination of *'multiple* ([b]) elements + that *lift up* ([u]) the *body* ([t])'. What's particularly interesting is that the idea of 'plurality' associated with this term suggests a connection not just to human feet but also to the limbs of the entire animal kingdom. This once again underscores how our ancient ancestors perceived humanity as just one part of the larger natural world.

The Kyrgyz verb өп [œp], meaning *to kiss (swiftly)*, can be deciphered as the act of a *'multitude* [p] + of *prompt rises* [œ]. 'As discussed in Volume I, its Proto-Indo-European counterpart *yeb^h- finds resonance in Ancient Greek, Sanskrit, Proto-Taharian, Luwian and Hittite.

This connection further highlights the shared ancestral roots of these words and the profound linguistic links between Kyrgyz, English, Latin, and pre-Proto-Indo-European languages. As discussed in Volume I, numerous Kyrgyz words offer more tangible connections to Ancient Latin or even Ancient Greek and pre-Greek terms that have widely migrated to other Proto-Indo-European (PIE) daughter languages.

As detailed discussions of the related linguistic links were provided in the previous volume, please refer to that volume for further information.

Here are some examples of terms from ancient Indo-European languages and their corresponding Kyrgyz counterparts, which closely match in meaning.

- Hittite:
  - h_2 and h_3 are pronounced as [q] in Kyrgyz, similar to Hittite.
  - Hittite *attas* vs. Kyrgyz [ata]
  - Hittite *annas* vs. Kyrgyz [ana]
  - Hittite *illuyanka* vs. Kyrgyz [jɯlän]
  - Hittite *tezzi* vs. Kyrgyz [de]
  - Hittite *as* vs. Kyrgyz [al]
  - Hittite *wēs* and *sumēs* vs. Kyrgyz [biz] and [siz]

- Pre-Greek substratum:
  - *ko.lo'sos* vs. Kyrgyz [qolos]

- Ancient Greek:
  - *Argos* vs. Kyrgyz [ar-gœz]
  - *energy (en+ergon)* vs. Kyrgyz [ergi]
  - *pan-* vs. Kyrgyz [paɴ]
  - *archon* vs. Kyrgyz [arqa]
  - *anchor* vs. Kyrgyz [gœ:kœr]

- Etruscan and Kyrgyz share numerous linguistic characteristics and exhibit a multitude of mirroring words (over 40 listed in Volume I). Examples of words suggested to be of Etruscan origin in English include *antenna, April, arena, atrium, belt, military, market, mundane, palace, person, Rome, satellite, Triumph, and Vernacular.*

- Latin:
  - *election (eligere)* vs. [ele] and [elek]
  - *turris* vs. [tür].

LITERACY VS. ORALITY

The culture's ability to retain its original structure can be attributed to its prolonged isolation and independent evolution. This is the case with Kyrgyz culture, which is characterized by a high-altitude semi-nomadic life-style and limited to specific uses of writing .

This phenomenon draws parallels with the concept of the *Inner Asia Mountains Corridor* (Refer to the Volume I for the details), emphasizing the pivotal role that semi-nomadic communities within mountainous regions played in disseminating prehistoric technological advancements across the vast expanse of Eurasia.

Caption of the Chapter Opening Image (Fig. 4): The Primordial Calendar Circle. (Source: Public Domain. See List of Figures)

This reconstruction of an archaeoastronomical device, the Calendar Circle, originates from the archeological site dating back to more than 10,000 years ago. It is one of the numerous sites that attests to the early humans' substantial understanding of astronomy long before the invention of writing.

"E Pur Si Muove" ("And Yet It Moves") [42]

Indeed, the span of orality extends far beyond the horizon of recorded history, a realm largely shrouded in mystery and accessible primarily through fragments preserved by archeological discoveries and genetic insights. Modern perceptions, often influenced by our literacy-centric world, can inadvertently underestimate the depth and significance of this ancient era. The assumption that prehistory lacked significant breakthroughs or intellectual milestones contradicts the very nature of human curiosity and ingenuity. It's important to recognize that scientific knowledge did not miraculously materialize on the day it was first transcribed onto parchment.

For instance, the field of astronomy did not spring into existence with the first notation of star names (Refer to Fig. 3).

The knowledge encoded in the epic *Manas* reflects a remarkable grasp of geography, a testament to a comprehensive understanding that predated the act of writing. The Kyrgyz term *төгөрөктүн төрт бурчу'*,' meaning *'four corners of the sphere,'* hints at an ancient Kyrgyz understanding of the Earth's spherical shape and its four cardinal directions. This concept reflects deep-rooted knowledge of the world's geometry and directionality.

Counting systems, intricately woven into cultures, existed long before the advent of written numerals.

In the Kyrgyz language, echoes of an advanced understanding of human anatomy are embedded within its terminology, revealing a depth of knowledge that preceded formal documentation.

All of the musical instruments and sport games of our era arose from prehistoric times.

The invention of such a technological masterpiece in construction, like the yurt, occurred chiliads of years before the invention of writing.

The lens through which we view prehistoric achievements shapes our perception. Deep within the nuanced and embryonic words of our primordial language, we discern a profound emphasis on internal understanding, purpose, and self-knowledge. Their developmental trajectory seemingly prioritized an exploration of the self and the greater purpose of existence, rather than being fixated solely on material gains—the trappings of a literate society.

Prehistoric Communication Modes And Literacy

The evolution of human thought encompasses more than just the development of sophisticated oral language. It begins with a language of gestures, tactile cues, and primal vocalizations. This non-verbal mode of communication likely played a crucial role for our ancient ancestors, allowing them to interact without attracting the attention of predators in their dangerous and untamed environments. Orality is just one facet of the many communication modalities that preceded subsequent form of expression—literacy.

In a broader context, early human communication can be divided into two main categories: sound-based and visual-based.

Sound-based communication includes not only verbal language but also other forms like clapping and the use of musical instruments.

Visual-based communication encompasses gestures,

dance, petroglyphs, and other methods of crafting visual narratives. These communication modalities can be associated with either orality or literacy based on the tangible or intangible forms in which they are produced and preserved.

Within the framework of this book, these communication modes can also be categorized as *historic* or *prehistoric* based on the logic of literacy, which often defines historic periods as those with tangible written records.

However, there is also a transitional layer that corresponds to "prehistoric-like" or the *"primary-oral-like,"* covering communication that is produced in a nontangible way but preserved in a tangible form. Examples of this transitional layer include early Vedic texts showing signs of "being of oral source," records of verses of the epic *Manas*—the oral "encyclopaedia", recorded texts of *Aitysh* (an improvisational singing contest) and music of folk instruments like *komuz* being recorded in notations.

This categorization helps us to understand the richness and diversity of human communication throughout history and how it has evolved from *prehistoric* modes to ones of literacy.

The case of non-verbal communication, such as the language of dance, provides an interesting perspective on the evolution of human expression.

Taking the Kyrgyz word for dance, бий [bij], we can decode its initial, oral-like form. This word is constructed from the phonemes we discussed in the earlier chapter. The [b] in бий relates to the *plurality*, while the combination [ij] signifies *bending*. Therefore, the core meaning of the term is to translate as *multiple bending*. In its "prehistoric" form, dance would have simply been a form of self-bending, a non-verbal expression of movement and emotion.

This early form of dance gets further depicted through petroglyphs or other tangible means like the decoration on the prehistoric piece of ceramic (Fig. 5), signifying the era of its *primary oral-likeness*.

Fig. 5. Prehistoric Dancers (circa 5000 BC). (Source: Public Domain. See List of Figures)

This ceramic artifact, adorned with dancing figurines, dates back to a time thousands years before the development of writing.

As societies evolved and literacy became more prevalent, dance moved from its orality-like form to a standardized, "written down" form. Dance moves were recorded with detailed pictures and descriptions, allowing for precise replication and transmission, particularly in the context of sport disciplines or formal dance styles.

Music, as a distinct form of human communication,

follows a developmental trajectory similar to other forms of expression. It can be categorized into stages that align with the transition from orality to literacy too:

1. **Orality-Like Stage**: The origins of music can be traced back to our ancestors' attempts to imitate the sounds of nature. In this early stage, music was likely produced using simple instruments or vocalizations to mimic natural sounds. This form of music was part of the oral tradition, passed down through generations.

2. **Primary Oral-Like Stage**: As human societies developed, so did their musical abilities. Music in this stage involved the use of instruments that were not yet designed for notation but already categorized in the groups that jointly could make an *prehistoric* orchestra. Such type of music continues to be an integral part of oral traditions and rituals, where Kyrgyz *komuz* still places a role.

3. **Literacy in Music**: The transition to literacy in music marked a significant shift. This stage involved the development of a written musical notation system to represent melodies, rhythms, and harmonies. To meet this purpose, the musical instruments were also "enhanced" by features to provide fixed tuning and sounds. Composers and musicians could now create music directly on paper, allowing for more precise replication of musical pieces.

Throughout these stages, music remained a fundamental mode of human expression, evolving in tandem with the broader shift from orality to literacy. While the development of written music has certainly facilitated the preservation and dissemination of musical compositions, enriching human culture and artistic expression, it has also led to a decline in improvisation and non-standardized tones.

Singing, even though it's a technique that uses

the speech organs, likely existed long before the first meaningful sounds were produced by early humans. The Kyrgyz term for singing, ыр [ɯr], indicates that it had a primordial structure and meaning. It can be understood as '*proximity* [ɯ] + *covering* [r],' suggesting that it originally consisted of prolonged, emotionally rich sounds with no specific meaning, intended to be heard within nearby vicinity.

Over time, singing evolved into a feature of oral culture with attached meanings and musical accompaniment. In its *primary-oral-like* stage, it combined the oral text with music, much like recording an initially oral tradition. The *literacy-like* form of singing, on the other hand, is based on pre-written text set to music.

Another form of expression was symbolism. In its *oral-like* form, it consisted of conveying messages with minimal resources. For instance, the Kyrgyz *Ak-kalpak*, the national head ware discussed in Volume I, symbolizes the divine realm of snow-covered peaks, the spherical shape of the Earth, and its four cardinal directions.

Prehistoric *kurgans* (*коргон* [qorgon] in Kyrgyz), traditionally understood as large burial sites [45] or ruins of monumental structures in Kyrgyz [46], stand as enduring symbols of the ancient power. Their consistent structure suggests a form of standardization in prehistoric times, reflecting a stage of early symbolic development, reminiscent of a *primary-oral* culture.

In contrast, ancient pyramids, shaped like mountains and representing rulers' might, are examples of *literacy-like* symbolism, as they were built based on preliminary paperwork. They were also enormously resource consuming.

By acknowledging the substantial intellectual legacy of the oral tradition, we recalibrate our understanding of human progress. The knowledge and wisdom amassed during epochs of orality laid the foundation for subsequent achievements, often influencing the trajectory of knowledge dissemination and cultural evolution. It is within the labyrinth of orality that we discover the roots of not only language but also the roots of scientific inquiry, innovation, and the intricate tapestry of human thought.

Comparing orality and literacy, as well as orality-like and literacy-like communication modes, offers valuable insights into the unique characteristics and cultural outcomes associated with each form.

Let's summarize some highlighted key points:

1. **Spontaneity vs. "Within the Box"**: Orality and orality-like modes allow for spontaneous creativity and improvisation, often pushing boundaries. Literacy and literacy-like modes are more likely to adhere to established frameworks and conventions, staying "within the box."

2. **Versatility vs. Specialization**: Orality and orality-like modes are versatile and adaptable. They can encompass a wide range of expressions, from storytelling to dance to music, often blurring boundaries between them. Literacy and literacy-like modes, on the other hand, tend to specialize in specific forms of expression, with distinct rules and structures.

3. **Philosophical Vagueness vs. Practical Precision**: Orality often carries a sense of philosophical vagueness, where interpretations may be long and meanings can be layered. In contrast, literacy emphasizes practical precision, with clear definitions, standardized rules, and reduced ambiguity.

4. **Wholistic vs. Narrowly Focused**: Orality and orality-like modes view the communicator as an integral part of nature and the universe as a whole, whereas literacy

and literacy-like modes tend to differentiate between humans and the non-human or between "old" and "new" worlds.

5. **Egalitarian vs. Egocentric**: Orality-driven communication is oriented towards creating collective value (*Kym/Kut*) for others, while literacy often encourages a more self-centered focus on personal gain.

6. **Minimalist vs. Maximalist**: Orality, being rooted in nature, typically utilizes available resources efficiently. In contrast, literacy seeks diverse resources to fulfill its ambitions more expansively.

7. **Strait and Open vs. Indirect and Veiled**: Oral and orality like modes of expression aimed directly to the receivers, so having limitations in being veiled, while literacy thoughts being first boiled inside and then put on paper (According to legend, the Kyrgyz people abandoned their written language after suffering a devastating defeat, brought about by their trust in the contents of an enemy's letter).

By recognizing these distinctions, we can gain a deeper understanding of how different modes of communication shape cultural outcomes and human consciousness.

Orality, for instance, functions as an improvised mode of communication, shared among many individuals and often recorded solely within our minds. It is expressed in ways conducive to memorization.

In contrast, literacy hinges on individual apprehension, unaided by immediate external input, thereby allowing for comprehensive comprehension or potential misconstrual of the subject matter. Moreover, literacy encapsulates this comprehension in a tangible format, facilitating subsequent input and interpretations free from temporal constraints.

Comparing the vivid idiomatic expressions of orality with the precise terms of literacy illustrates the discussed differences in the quality of the two. Consider the Kyrgyz expression *'shear the skewbald sheep separately'* (Davletbakova, 19), which precisely denotes the modern international term of Latin origin, *'discrimination.'* While the first one is longer, it is easy to say and memorize due to its simplicity and association with everyday life of the ancient pastoral societies. On the other hand, the second one is shorter but more challenging to pronounce and remember for an unfamiliar person, as it is derived from an unfamiliar stem. The first expression is colorful, fun, and versatile, while the second is precise and used specifically in the context of people's relationships.

This evolution, from orality to literacy, has, in my perspective, not only distanced humanity from its common language (as retold in the first volume's Babel tower story), but it has also influenced our evolving perception of yoga. It has transitioned from an ancient emphasis on mindfulness to a contemporary portrayal encompassing aspects of "acrobatic" or even *beer-drinking yoga* [78].

ORAL MIND

The absence of the imperative to craft a verbally memorable message inherent in literacy has yielded more precise and pragmatic communication, mitigating the ambiguity often prevalent in more philosophically inclined oral discourse.

Notably, we observe that while the orthography of historically alphabetic written cultures engenders the fixation of specifically spelled standalone words with distinct meanings, primary oral cultures exhibit words that can harbor several entirely disparate meanings contingent upon their contextual companions.

Caption of the Chapter Opening Image (Fig. 6): The Rainbow Arc–A Celestial Symbol of the Divine Sky. (Source: Public Domain. See List of Figures)

The rainbow arc, stretching across the horizon, can be interpreted as a symbolic representation of the all-encompassing sky, known as *Көк* [kœk] in Kyrgyz. This notion of the sky as an overarching presence may have influenced the use of *Көк* as one of the names for God in Kyrgyz culture.

"Connecting The Dots..."

The "primary oral" Sanskrit root words often present challenges for translation due to their polysemic nature. A single word can have numerous, sometimes conflicting, meanings, and a given meaning may be represented by multiple distinct words. This phenomenon is particularly evident when translating concepts like *white* or the individual words like *bala* from Sanskrit to English.

The color *white*, for example, is rendered in Sanskrit using various terms with distinct phonetic patterns. Similarly, *bala* can refer to a multitude of meanings, including *child*, *strength*, and *army* [79]. This polysemy is surprising for a root language like Sanskrit, especially from a "literate" perspective, which often views it as having minimal external borrowings.

Interestingly, some of the Sanskrit terms for the color *white* (*acala*) and the meanings of *bala* used in the names of multiple deities' *sons* have corresponding equivalents in Kyrgyz. For instance, while Sanskrit *acala bala* is used to name Shiva, Kyrgyz агала бала [agala bala] would means '*a whitish son.*' Other examples include: *ahar* (for a white day in Sanskrit) and the Kyrgyz verb агар [agar] (to become white); the Kyrgyz word күү [qü] (used as color *white* to describe visual characteristics of people and animals, as discussed in Volume I) and Sanskrit terms like *kuvalayam* (white lotus), *kumud* (white lily), and *gaura* (white mustard).

Curiously both, ак [aq] for *white* and бала [bala] for a *son*, where discussed in relation to the Sumerian King *Aga/Ak-Kaz* (white goos) in the Volume I.

An example of a Kyrgyz term denoting multiple seemingly unrelated meanings would be the word кат [qat], which may signify (to) *hide* (something) or (to) *stay awake*, (to) *attach* or (to) *stale* and the *layer*. Only by looking at it through the prism of the proto-terms can we understand the connections. Deciphering the word gives us a broader connotation of the 'the *land/place* [q] + *elevated/above* [a] + *entity/body* [t]. 'Correspondingly, the more narrow meanings can be interpreted as '*landing/placing* [q] something + *high* (or on *top*) [a] + over (of) the *body* [t]' for the act of *hiding*, '*keeping* (as an act of placing) [q] + a *body* [t] *up* [a]' for (to) *stay awake* over night, and '*placing* [q] + *entity* (presumably food) [t] + on *top* [a] (of each other)' is to a result of in appearance of the *layers* and the food being piled in layers is naturally to connect to the notion of things getting *attached* and growing *stale*.

In a similar vein, examining Kyrgyz words for (to) *warm up*, жылы [dʒɯlɯ], жылаң [dʒɯlaŋ] for *naked*, and жылаажын [dʒɯlädʒɯn] for *bell for the prey bird*, it might seem perplexing that they may share the same root, жыл [dʒɯl], which means (to) *move* or *the year*. However, when viewed in the context of oral development and the prehistoric ur-vocabulary, these connections become clearer. We can hypothesize that our ancestors, already equipped with a term for (to) *move (жыл)*, recognized that friction, generated by the movement of objects against each other, produces heat. Consequently, they derived a term for (to) *warm up (жылы)*. Similarly, having a term for a *snake*, жылаан [dʒɯlän] also deriving from the same stem *(жыл)*, as discussed earlier (in Volume I), they coined the term for *naked* to signify being without fur, akin to a snake. Furthermore, now equipped with utterances with meaning of (to) *move* and being of a *snake-like appearance*, the progenitors came up with the name for a bell for the raptor, reflecting its properties as being *snake-shiny* and *signaling the movement*, with a more complex connotation.

These orality-induced "ambiguities" also surface when

translating Kyrgyz words into languages characterized by elaborate literacy. Consider the term *кара* [qara]: when employed as an adjective, it can denote *black* as a color along with its associated implications. Yet, as a noun, it assumes one a single *cattle*, or may even allude to *literacy* itself. Morphing into a verb, it shape-shifts into the imperative *have a look*. When integrated into compound words, it endows the primary word with connotations of *real*, *veritable*, *proper*, *natural* or *the only one*. Conversely, when positioned at a word's terminus, it imparts an essence of being a constituent of a larger ensemble.

Moreover, the given names in general, and the toponyms in particular, follow the logic of denoting certain desired or existing qualities of the subject, often revealing multiple layers of information about the place of different backgrounds.

A prime example of such a geographical name is Altai, as discussed earlier. On one hand, it denotes a wilderness where, upon the arrival of Kyrgyz people, canine animals dominated. On another hand, it signifies the length of the exodus trip from the ancestral land.

The name for the Kyrgyz nation itself, along with the names of other nations within the conglomerate of Turkic peoples, offers compelling examples too.

The term *Түрк* [tyrk] 'bulky, 'which in Kyrgyz corresponds to both *Turkic people* in general and separately *Turks*, serving as the root for the adjective *түркүн* [tyrkyn] '*diverse/various*, 'suggests the connotation of a union of many diverse nations, similar to today's EU. Historically, this union also included people of the Mongolian descent with whom *Turkic people* share common history and traditions, rooted in common ancestry of *Xiongnu* [47] as discussed in the Volume I.

The notion of *diversity* among the Turkic people of today is well visible in the variety of nations representing the people of today's Turkey–the biggest nation within the group. As the diagram below shows, the results of the genetic studies vividly demonstrate a very diverse composition among the Y-DNA samples of today's Turkey (Refer to Fig. 7).

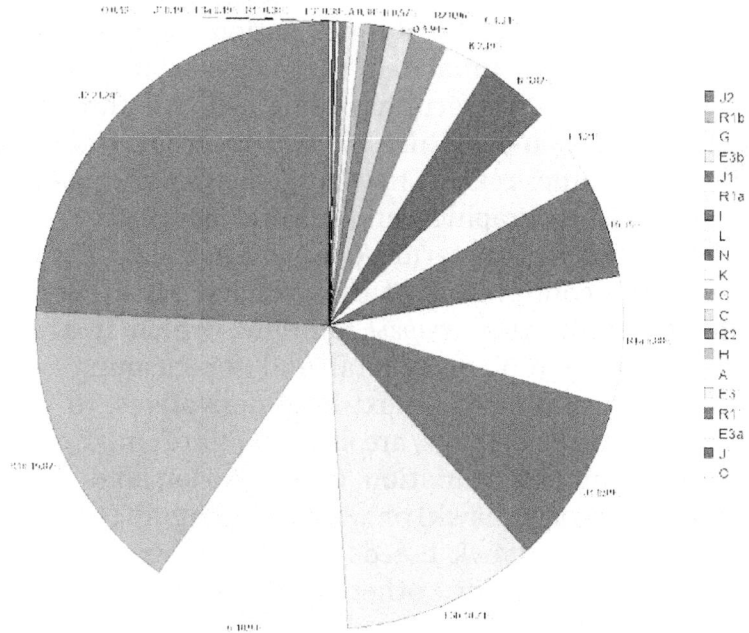

Fig. 7: Y-DNA distribution in present day Turkey. (Source: Public Domain. See List of Figures)

This pie chart vividly illustrates the diverse genetic composition of Turkey's modern population. This diversity aligns with the historical openness of Turkic peoples, who were known for forming alliances with other nations. As discussed in the first volume of this book, the nomadic alliances to the east of Ancient Greece referred to themselves as *Turken*—a term closely resembling the Kyrgyz word *tyrkyn*, meaning "diverse"—and were similarly known in Greek as the *Tyrrhenians*.

The names within that union also sound like adjectives: *Алтай* [altaj] –an *apex predator* (as the key core nation within the conglomerate?), *Каракалпак* [qaraqalpaq] –a *black hat* (emphasizing distinction from the white-hatted Kyrgyz people?), *Моңол* [moŋol] *–distinct* (by language?), *Өзбек* [œzbek] *–self-reliable*, *Уйгур* [ujgur] *–restless*, *Татар* [tatar] *–one who is to taste* (hinting at the nation's rich cuisine), and so on.

From this perspective, with its root *кыр* [qɯr] meaning *ridge*, the name of the Kyrgyz nation signifies people who have always inhabited the ridges—'*the mountain-dwelling people.*' This term has remained true throughout Kyrgyz history and prehistory, and together with other considered names reflects how language can encapsulate a community's geographical and cultural identity.

Additionally, the term *Кыргыз* [qɯrgɯz] naturally inherits the connotation of the primary derivative word from the stem (*кыр*) *кыргы* [qɯrgɯ], which is a name for a scraping tool in general and for cleaning a gun barrel in particular. The next-level derivatives, to which the name Kyrgyz belongs, are *кыргын* [qɯrgɯn], referring to the act of extermination or its owner, and *кыргый* [qɯrgɯj] (sparrow-hawk) or *кыргыек* [qɯrgɯj] (goshawk), the names for a hawk breeds known for its remarkable efficiency in hunting other birds, often giving the impression of complete annihilation during its attacks. Both terms, while continuing the narrative provided by their root, symbolize the act of total elimination of the object by the subjects they represent.

Furthermore, as already discussed, the suffix -*з* [z] imparts a sense of restraint in the act described by the stem. From this perspective, the term *кыргыз* conveys the connotation of '(a nation) *never engaging in the annihilation* (of others),' reflecting restraint in action.

A similar effect of this suffix is evident in the word for the *star*, *жылдыз* [dʑɯldɯz], which, being a derivative of the verb *жыл* [dʑɯl], meaning (to) *move*. The past tense form *жылды* [dʑɯldɯ], when suffixed by -*з*, creates connotation of an object *'without movement.'* Although this interpretation aligns with the concept of stationary stars, it raises the curious question: did prehistoric people understand that it was the Earth moving and not the stars? This question goes alongside another cosmic Altaic term *ай-аяс* [ajajaz], which, while meaning *universe*, can be literally translated as *moon-freezing*. Could this possibly hint at the knowledge of freezing temperature of outer space by the ancients?

Returning to the term Kyrgyz, intriguingly, both aspects, the ridge living and non-aggressiveness, embedded in the quality of the term Kyrgyz evoke memories of the peaceful, mountainous civilization of the Indus Valley. Such quality within the name is also affirmed by another adage translated as: *'If a nation joins with others, it is Kut; if a nation separates from another, it is a calamity.'* Indeed, a deep dive into a language's morphology, phonetics, and structure can unveil valuable insights into the way of life, environment, and heritage of its speakers.

The name Kyrgyz is simple, precise, and practical, serving as a guiding principle for the people of the subject nation, while also possessing a deep philosophical dimension, showcasing the power of orality once again. An illustration of this concept emerges from the Kyrgyz language, where precision is achieved by orchestrating either a word's placement within a sentence or its incorporation into compound words. Alternatively, clarity can be inherently embedded in the foundational structure of root words themselves.

The intricacy of these multifarious connotations and the inherent malleability of the Kyrgyz language make its translation into languages entrenched in literacy a formidable task. Much like Sanskrit, it requires the encapsulation of the labyrinthine subtleties and manifold interpretations that epitomize oral expression.

Focus On Wellness

The multi-purpose nature, which in literacy can be interpreted as the "meaninglessness" of certain words in a language, often holds fascinating insights.

Consider the Kyrgyz word *coo* [sɒ:], which encapsulates a dual meaning, referring to both a *living being* and being in *good health* (in a proper state of living?). Given its construction and insights from the sections of the book, we can now decode *coo* as 'the state of being *on the surface* [s] + of *mortals 'realm* [ɒ:],' which corresponds with the both connotations signifying being *alive* in general.

Interestingly, the English term *soul*, of uncertain origin [46], which contains phoneme [l] signifying *adhesion*, shares a remarkable linguistic resemblance to Kyrgyz [sɒ:]. Now we understand its meaning as 'one that *holds* [l] us + on the *surface* [s] + of the *mortal realm* [ɒ:],' which refers to the a of *wellness* too.

It is also noteworthy that the old version of *soul*—*sawol*, sound almost identical to the return greeting in Kyrgyz that similarly wishes *wellness*—*coo бол!* [sɒ:bol], denoting '*be alive and in good health!*'

The Kyrgyz word for *dance,* which encapsulates the idea of *self-bending* (discussed before), offers a glimpse into how primary oral language employs ingenious methods to convey precise meaning.

Its core connotation effectively delivers two seemingly disparate noun meanings of *lord* and *dance*. While the former can be interpreted as 'one to whom *many* [b] people + *bend* [ij],' the latter corresponds to the notion of a '*complex* [b] + of *self-bending* [ij] moves.'

Fig. 8. Kyrgyz Dance Filmed in 1924. (Continued from Volume I, Source: Public Domain. See List of Figures and Bibliography for the reference to the YouTube video)

The film fragments reveal movements in the Kyrgyz dance that resemble a form of stretching practice. Unlike the typical bending seen in many dance styles, some of these movements appear to focus on stretching the spinal cord and various body parts, giving the dance a unique "unnatural" physicality.

Remarkably, despite being steeped in oral culture, Kyrgyz lacked a distinct dance tradition. Instead, the only form of dance known among the Kyrgyz of "Radlov's time" consisted of a series of stretching-like maneuvers referred to as *Кыргыз бий* [quɪrgɯz bij] translating as '*Kyrgyz dance*' or *Кара-жорго* [qara dʒɒrgɒ]–*Veritable amble* (See Fig. 8, above), where second stem denotes flowing move in general.

Kyrgyz folklore often associates the ideal horse with a bird of prey, and legendary heroes are depicted riding Pegasus-like steeds. This connection is reflected in the dance's rhythmic movements, which mimic the flapping of wings and the trotting of a horse. The dance's flowing nature and arm movements bear a striking resemblance to certain yogic practices. Like any dance, this "oral-like" bodily expression mirrors the fluidity and embodiment of spoken language itself.

Interestingly, when we connect two earlier discussed phrases, '*the husband knows his raptor, while the wife knows her work*' and '*the first treasure is health,*' it suggests that the former statement may also refer to the Kyrgyz dancing practice. Such interpretation would shed light on some potentially confusing and distant aspects of ancient society such as:

a) there was only one dance, predominantly performed by men;

b) the dance moves were meant to be flowing and reminiscent of the flight of the prey bird;

c) the term for dance encompassed a set of self-bending exercises, possibly designed to maintain good physical condition; and,

d) the name for the cerebellum, *каракуш* [qaraquş], involved the word for *prey bird* (*куш* [quş]), possibly indicating the energy residing there that facilitates the movement of consciousness within and outside the body. This revelation hints at the logic of "flying" focus through the anatomy of body and to the cosmos, as will be discussed in the related chapter. Moreover, such understanding of the first statement is evident because not every family, even in the ancient times of a simple life amidst the mountains, would have had a raptor for entertainment and engagement, which otherwise would draw a parallel with our ubiquitous modern companions—the smartphone and computer.

Absolutely, granting due credit to our prehistoric ancestors is a vital aspect of understanding the remarkable legacy they left for us. Their cognitive abilities, while existing in the same or perhaps even larger capacities as today, were not confined to mere sustenance tasks. The ancestral brain was an intricate reservoir of potential, harnessed for purposes beyond the immediate demands of survival. In fact, one could speculate that their utilization of brainpower was even more efficient than our modern practices.

In light of the premise that embryonic human speech inherently carries connotations linked to the anatomy of their articulation, it is unsurprising that our proto-human ancestors merged their analytical and linguistic faculties to explore their own bodies. It's reasonable to assume that the naming of our most conspicuous body parts transpired during an early phase of linguistic development.

This supposition finds further support in the widespread tendency to derive verbs from the names of body organs: *handling* from *hand* or *heading* from *head*. This notion is substantiated by examples of anatomical terms in their most elemental two-phoned form, such as Latin *os* [ɒs] for *mouth,* English *eye,* and Kyrgyz *уч* [itɕ] for *abdomen,* among numerous others.

While we often attribute specific meanings to anatomical terms, as observed in the Kyrgyz language, it's noteworthy that certain organs, despite their complex names and potential for derivative terms, lack inherent meaning. Viewing this terminology through the lens of orality suggests that organ names were designed to be multifunctional, much like the qualities of words in primary oral languages in general. This phenomenon of polysemy is apparent throughout the text of this book.

The Kyrgyz anatomical terminology often incorporates specific vibrating sounds that align with the location, proximity, and structural composition of these organs. This concept hints at a correspondence between the vibrations generated by the production of particular sounds and specific areas within the body. In this sense, these organ names might have served as early forms of mantras.

From this perspective, it becomes apparent that the naming of organs served multiple purposes, including conveying their position within the body. Moreover, when examined in the context of practices such as yoga, Kyrgyz-Altai voiced uvular trill singing, and Kyrgyz linguistics, this linguistic feature provides subtle insights into concepts like 'mantras,' 'tantras,' and 'chakras.'

The above feature of the language, along with wisdom of Kyrgyz folk medicine in general shares intriguing parallels with *Ayurveda*, "the yogic medicine." Both traditions share a fundamental belief in attributing the human body with an innate energy and emphasize the vital importance of preserving a harmonious balance within this energy. The term *Ayurveda*, its core principle of *Dosha*, and other yogic terminology will be explored in greater depth in the upcoming chapter of this book (in Part 2 of this Volume). It's captivating to observe that the etymology of these terms in Kyrgyz appears to resonate with related meanings, further illustrating the interconnectivity of linguistic expressions across diverse cultures.

Short Words–Deep Meanings

The linguistic features of humanity's ur-language discussed in the previous chapters are also remarkable for how our proto-human ancestors managed to embed something philosophically profound within the few phoned rudimentary words. These simple words, with their basic phonetic compositions, carried deep meanings and insights into early human consciousness and the way they perceived the world around them. The immediate derivatives of those "primitive" terms are even more astonishing.

For instance, the aforementioned Kyrgyz verb э [e] signifying an existence can be seen as the initial term for a life itself. Enhanced by the morpheme for continuous growth, [s], it yields эс [es], which now creates a significant philosophical term for consciousness or mind with the connotation of '*infinite and evolving* [s] + *existence* [e]'—a subtle allusion to the ceaseless cycle of non-physical life. Additionally, the stem э is notably present in words for crucial survival-related actions, such as эм [em] for (to) *suck* (the breast) and эт [et] for *meat*, a vital sustenance for the early hunter-gatherer ancestors.

Structure of the word for (to) *die*, өл [œl], suggests that early people saw this event as a '*prompt rise* [œ] + to *join/ glue* [l].' From this, we can deduce that even then, they believed in the existence of a universal matter above to which the эс [es] (soul) connects in the afterlife.

Another primordial in its structure word, уу [ü] for *poison*, seen as opposed in meaning to у [u] for (to) *hover*, indicates how it is perceived as affecting a person—making them *'falling down.'* With the addition of the suffix [-z], its derivative *ууз* [üz] for *colostrum* suggests to have properties that counteract or reduce poisoning.

Consider how early ancestors viewed food, the essence that derives from the reinterpreting Kyrgyz term for it—*аш* [aʃ]. By analyzing its composition, we can "translate" it as *'visible/high up* ([a]) + *together* ([ʃ]),*' which can be interpreted as *'hanging up for all of us.'* This interpretation aligns with how people in the earliest societal form of gatherers might have perceived food—as the hanging *up* berries and fruits that are collected and consumed *together*. What adds to the intrigue is that other meanings of this term support this notion: the first meaning is precisely the *consumable wild berries*; the second meaning is the *first death anniversary gathering* for commemoration; and another meaning is *to surplus* or the act of *outrunning*, exceeding (as being *above*) what is *jointly* considered as sufficient or a norm.

The case of the Kyrgyz term *кыз* [quɯz], which signifies total restriction of force, as briefly touched upon before, perfectly reflects Kyrgyz cultural values that hold daughters and girls in high esteem. This simple three-phoned word has managed to instill profound respect for young ladies and women in general in Kyrgyz society, a feat that written laws often struggle to achieve.

An adage further underscores the significance attributed to this term. The statement *'Кыздын кырк чачы уулу,'* which translates to *'Nothing is more respectful than a daughter's fourth hairs'* (referring to a specific girls' hairstyle), functions as a cultural law in primary oral society. It emphasizes the esteemed status of girls and the importance of treating them with the utmost respect and care.

Interestingly, if we break down this word as [q] + [ɯz], the term's connotation also reflects father's deep tenderness for his daughter, suggesting '(my little precious) *enduring noisiness* [ɯz] in the *immediate vicinity* [q].' This exemplifies the profound interplay of deep compound meanings and values encapsulated within a simple word consisting of just three sounds.

Exploring how the conciseness of orality forms complex philosophical terms from rudimentary words, let's once again revisit the "two-morphemed" *ap* [ar]. As discussed, this stem itself already carries a complex philosophical meaning, signifying *faraway*, *various*, and *wear out*. Together, these meanings offer the notion of the *horizon* as an edge between the real world and the afterlife.

The same two-phoned combination, although in reverse order, is present in the name of Egyptian Sun God *Ra*. This name likely signified '*one above who covers a variety of all (everyone), from here to the horizon, in their current life and the afterlife!*' As notable, this broader sense of meaning resonates with the connotations of the Kyrgyz word *ap*.

Interestingly, the interpretation of this term with the prolonged vowel offers a clear understanding of its opposite connotation. In this case, the opposite meaning would be something that is '*very narrow and beneath.*' This notion is closely reflected in the Kyrgyz term that also was touched upon before, *aap* [är], which translates to *pressed down ornaments, hand lines*, and the *fine lines of the face*.

The term *ar* is rich in philosophical meaning as reflected in its derivatives. When combined with the noun suffix -ка [qa], it forms *арка* [arqa] meaning *spine*. This term symbolizes *power, leadership*, and *support* or *protection*. By adding the adjective-forming suffix -кы [quɯ], it becomes *аркы* [arquɯ], meaning *distant*, and is often used to refer to the *afterlife* [75]. Curiously, both [arqa] and [arquɯ] share the stem [arq]. This stem is notably similar to one of the Ancient Greek word *archon*, meaning *leader* or *ruler*, said to be of uncertain origin [76]. From *archon* comes the term *archangel*, which also carries connotations of *protection* and belonging to the "*afterlife* location," mirroring the meanings found in Kyrgyz.

These connotations of the stem are also evident when *ар* suffixed by -*ба* [ba], which introduces a restrictive element. The term *арба'!* [arba] (48) is still used in Kyrgyz as a traditional greeting, expressing well-wishes for the recipient to stay full of life and not become weary.

Now, it's intriguing to note that this same morpheme [ar] appears to be the root of the name from Ancient Greek mythology, *Argos Panoptes, a many-eyed giant*, and there is no clear understanding of the origin of the name. However, when we examine it from the perspective of Kyrgyz linguistics, its phonological makeup aligns with *Ар-көз* [ar-gœz], meaning *many dissimilar eyes*, precisely describes the eponymous giant (as discussed in Volume I). Furthermore, the Kyrgyz *ar* and its derivative *apa* [ara], meaning *distance* and *archery aim*, demonstrate a clear linguistic connection to the English *arc* or *arch*. This connection extends further to the Latin *arcus*, meaning bow, and ultimately to the Proto-Indo-European root h_2erk^wos, also referring to a *bow* or *arrow* [77].

It is also worth mentioning that one of the options for the term *God* in Kyrgyz, *Теңир* [teɴir], provides a connotation similar to the interpretation of the Ancient Egyptian *Sun God Ra* (the reverse of *ar*). *Теңир*, whose Sumerian counterpart was *Dinir* [tiɴir], can be understood through its construction as a compound word. *Тең* [teɴ] signifies equality, *up* [ir] means *all together*, and

[r], considered separately, symbolizes *taking all over/ protecting*. Therefore, its meaning can be interpreted as *'one who covers/protects all together equally.'*

This interpretation sheds light on other name of the God in Kyrgyz, Көк [kœk], also meaning *sky*. Its structure suggests a similar connotation–'the matter that starts in one *place* [k/g] + *sharply elevates* [œ] + end descends in another *place* [k].' Such interpretations clearly draws the arc that covers all, a similar but notion of much bigger scale then rainbow (Refer to Fig. 6.).

Even more interesting is that its "vowel prolonged" counterpart with potentially reverse meaning, көөк [gœk] for the feminine pad (starting in one *place* [k/g], *sharply descending* [œ:] and elevates back at the *place* [k] on other end.' As discussed in the previous volume, this word show linguistic connection with the pre-Ancient Greek Proto-Indo-European word *$h_2$enk-ur-(ya-) [41].

In a similar vein, it's fascinating to observe that in Ancient Egyptian theology, the three primary aspects of the human soul are also constructed from two phones, bearing a resemblance to Kyrgyz counterparts [80]:

1. **Ka [ka]**, representing *'a life-force,'* might symbolize the *flow of life* in the earthly realm, echoing "two-morphemed" Kyrgyz composition ак [aq] for *to run/flow* (for the liquid) and, correspondingly, its connotation 'to flow from *high* up [a] + *to this place* [q]).

2. **Akh [aq]**, the quality of *'ka (a flow of* life) *of the afterlife,'* could symbolize the *flow* too, now directly akin to the Kyrgyz term ак from above where sound [q] is equal in pronunciation to the combination -*kh*.

3. **Ba [ba]**, associated with *'spiritual qualities that aid in the transition between ka and akh,'* may symbolize *many*

qualities that *elevate* the spirit between the Earth and heaven. In the primordial vocabulary's context, where [b] represents the concept of *us* and correspondingly *plurality*, [a] stands for *high up*, this interpretation seems to resonate. Furthermore, the reminiscent Kyrgyz word *бар* [bar], meaning '*to be present/exist*,' in particular in the context of the wish for the wellbeing *Бар бол!* ([bar bol]) covers all qualities being in "elevated" status of the life too.

Similar two-phoned divine terminology is also present in ancient Sumerian beliefs. As discussed previously, the name of the Earth goddess, *Ki*, as a compound word within the context of humanity's earliest one-sound vocabulary, can be understood as 'Goddess of everything *within* [i] *vicinity* [k].' Another name for the king of the gods was *An*, which can be decoded as '*One who* (as an object) [n] + is *Above* [a] all' [49].

These intriguing parallels between primeval Ancient Sumerian, Egyptian, Greek, and Kyrgyz philosophical terms serve as a testament to the shared human consciousness of expression, transcending linguistic and cultural disparities and geographical distances. They underscore the universality of certain fundamental human concepts and the profound ways in which our ancestors encoded them in their languages and cultures.

Kyrgyz term *yŭ* [yj] for *house* and (to) *pile/ pack* reflects the innate hunter-gatherers lifestyle of our remote ancestors, as discussed before. This word's dual meaning gives us insight into how they lived, picturing them as a group collecting food and piling it in their communal living space. It captures their perception of a place where they gathered and lived together, akin to a warehouse on one hand and a pack of predators on the other. The inclusion of the phoneme [j], symbolizing objects with *tapering edges/ ends*, offers an intriguing perspective on the structure of a place with the higher ceiling and *narrow* [y] entries, emphasizing the communal aspect of early human habitation.

The word *yŭ* has a broader connotation in its derivative *yŭγp* [yjyr] for *herd*, signifying *a family* or a group of animals.

Interestingly, both *yŭ* and the English word *pack* share a similar root meaning: the action of *piling things together*. This common root meaning gives rise to the secondary connotations of *family* or *herd* in both languages.

The linguistic phenomenon observed in this example, where the same deep meanings are encoded in phonetically distant words across languages, highlights the shared human consciousness of expression. This phenomenon transcends linguistic diversity and serves as a testament to the enduring commonalities in human thought.

The persistence of rudimentary two-phoned words in Kyrgyz folk names for various species offers a fascinating glimpse into the oral mindset too. Despite their brevity, these names often reveal a clear underlying logic, reminiscent of modern Latin binomial nomenclature, which employs descriptive terms [50].

While Latin for a domestic dog is *Canis lupus familiaris* denoting *Dog-Wolf-Domestic* [51], the Kyrgyz word, *um* [it], carries composition: [i] representing *internal* and [t] *entity*, symbolizing 'the *member* [i] + of the *human pack* [t] (as an *entity*).'

This concept remains relevant today, as in Kyrgyz tradition a breed of sighthound dog *taigan* (Fig. 25) is regarded not as ordinary dog but as a family member. It was the only breed to enter the house in the old times, reflecting the deep cultural significance in Kyrgyz society from the earliest stages of it joining the human pack.

Fig. 9. Kyrgyz taigan. (Source: Public Domain. See List of Figures)

The Kyrgyz taigan, a breed of dog renowned for its hunting prowess, has been a crucial companion to Kyrgyz people since ancient times. Along with trained Golden eagles, taigans played a vital role in providing sustenance for families.

The primordial structure of the Kyrgyz term aligns with archaeological findings, which dates the first domestication of dogs to the Altai region, the ancestral homeland of the Kyrgyz people, approximately 33,000 years ago.

Interestingly, the word [it] is similar in composition to the English word *it,* which is typically used to refer to a nearby object that can be pointed at. Both words contain the element [i] for *"inner circle" and* [t] for *object.* This analysis is also reflected in the Russian word *мы* [tɯ] (*you*) where [ɯ] signifies *intimate distance*, with overall connotation of the '*body* [t] + that is *intimately close* [ɯ].'

As mentioned before, the term for *horse* in Kyrgyz is *am* [at], composed of *'up'* and *'body/ structure,'* meaning 'it *lifts up* ([a]) + *the body* ([t]).' The sound used to summon a horse, which is also a two-phoned word *мо* [mɒ], can be interpreted as '*take me* [m] + *over* [ɒ].'

Kyrgyz word for *cow* is *уй* [uj], composed of [u] for *lifted up* and [j] for *protuberances*. This logically signifies 'it is with *lifted up protuberances (horns).*'

Similar connotation is also visible in the word for the sheep, *кой* [qoj], to be deciphered as '*protuberances* ([j]) + *above* ([o]) + *the ground* ([q]).' As this can be interpreted as 'one with the horns right above/ close to the ground, 'it hints on the "runty" animal when compared with the size of the cow.

The above animals were integral to early human communities. Derived from the call for the prey bird–*ку* [qu] ('*land* [q] *hovering* [u]) by its vowel prolonged, the word *куу* [qü], meaning *bird* (*not hovering but flying away* [ü] from here [q]) presents members of the animal kingdom that human consciousness has also deemed important since ancient times. This again demonstrates the origin of Kyrgyz words from the early human epoch.

Above *ку* [qu] gives rise to *куш* [quʂ], denoting the *prey bird* itself (a *partner* [ʂ] in *landing* [q] *hovering* [u] ones), such as the Golden eagle—the irreplaceable *taigan's* partner in hunting (see picture above, Fig. 10). The construction of this word carries the connotation of '*flying partner that lands the prey*,' reflecting a symbiotic relationship with humans.

This type of bird is philosophically perceived as occupying the highest rank in the animal kingdom's hierarchy, with humans somewhere lower.

Figure 10. Kyrgyz *Byrkytchy* and his Golden Eagle. (Source: Public Domain. See List of Figures. Also see Bibliography [Kokboru_YsykKol] for the reference on related YouTube video)

Eagle hunting is an ancient tradition in Kyrgyzstan. Considered the most prestigious form of falconry, eagle training has its own distinct profession, known as *бүркүтчү* [byrkytʧy]—*a man of the Eagles*.

The Kyrgyz term *куш-курт* [quʃ-qurt], directly translating as *bird*(of prey)-*worm*, for 'animal kingdom' reflects a hierarchical worldview similar to that of the Sumerian realm of gods and prey birds. This term implies a ranking of all animals from the highest (a falcon) to the lowest (worms).

The ancient Kyrgyz worldview placed humans, whom they considered "*wild-artiodactyla men*" (as discussed in Volume I), somewhere within this hierarchy. This suggests that they saw humans as part of the natural world, rather than above or below it.

Moreover, as discussed earlier, the term *ку* encompasses complex concepts like *Кут* [qut] and *Куда* [quda], with the connotations of *the one which bestows Кут upon* (God) and another very significant cultural term of, *co-father*, and its female version, *кудагый* [qudaguıj], *mother-in-law*. These figures are considered highly important in Kyrgyz tradition, with the corresponding words providing the connotation of a person *of Kym*—of only good relations.

Names Of The God

Absolutely, the evolution of divine names in Kyrgyz pre-Islamic beliefs provides a fascinating glimpse into the development of human language and thought. It's remarkable to see how these names progressed from simple, imitative terms to more complex and philosophical concepts, mirroring the intellectual and linguistic advancements of ancient societies. These names not only represented the evolving understanding of the divine but also reflected the cultural and historical context in which they emerged.

Based on its brevity, we can infer that the earliest name for the God might have been the morpheme *O* [ɒ], a symbol that has transcended millennia and continues to exist in modern Kyrgyz as an adverb of *the air, the matter above us*. It is mostly used in combination with the terms signifying the world and refers to the realm of the *afterlife*. In the Kyrgyz old beliefs the afterlife was perceived more like a heaven, with no concept of hell, and located at the pinnacle of the universe. Correspondingly, if *o is used* as a name for God, and as today, accompanied by a gesture pointing upward, it is signifying *The One/Matter Above Us All*. This symbol *O* is a testament to the simplicity and profundity of ancient communication. In those distant days, language was an uncomplicated "dance" of gestures and basic sounds, direct and effective in its expression of profound ideas.

But as time flowed on, the speech bloomed with little more complexity. Prolonged vowels entered the stage. *O* now gets joined by Ээ [ë], a symbol for '*The Matter with Power Over All*,' which, to this day, also symbolizes the *owner* in general. The verbal abilities were evolving, and so was a perception of the divine. Still today, this term, as Эгем [egem] is used to say "*My Lord.*"

Then, with our common proto-human ancestors' speech organs 'ability to generate consonants, a new era was marked. Now, a new kind of term as a compound word entered the arena, bringing a new name for the God—*Көк* [gœk], meaning *The Sky*. Based on its makeup, as examined before, it encompassed 'everything that *falls down* [œ] *on Earth, from place* [g] *to place* [k]*, horizon to horizon,*' expanding comprehension of the divine.

Yet, life has its tumultuous moments. *The Great Flood* of ancient myths was one such cataclysm, marked by thunderous roars and storms of anger coming from above. This notion brought fear of God's wrath and ferocity expressed in a corresponding name for those times—*Буркан* [burkan], which is probably derived from its initial connotation of an onomatopoeic term echoing the rumbling thunder and the tempestuous rage. As covered in the Volume I, similar divine name was used by ancient Hittites too.

The time after chaos, which influenced humanity's consciousness, brought new interpretations in the understanding of human's purpose in life, giving rise to an entirely new kind of concept—blessing, represented by the term *Kym*, discussed before. From this philosophical notion, another word-name for God emerged, *Кудай* [quda] (as *Kut* + [aj], meaning *Kut-like*), which is commonly used to this day, that can be decoded as '*The One who bestows Kym— all goodness in life.*'

As consciousness advances and literacy emerges, we encounter the next name (still well preserved in Kyrgyz language) in the divine lexicon, one that hails from the times of early civilizations. This name is embodied in the term *Теңир* [teɴir], which encapsulates a more refined yet still profoundly philosophical understanding (discussed before). It symbolizes a divinity that is *'equalizes all'* and possesses the power *to cover and encompass all*, representing the omnipotence and omnipresence of the divine.

As literacy became widespread, the divine nomenclature evolved to embrace more pragmatic names. Among these, we find *Жараткан* [ʤaratqan], signifying *the Creator*, and *Жасаган* [ʤasagan], representing *the Maker*. These names reflect a shift towards a more practical and purpose-driven understanding of the divine.

While the concept of God was primarily associated with blessings and judgment, the responsibility of assisting humans with their daily affairs fell upon various divine patrons. Among them were figures like *Умай-эне* [umajene], known as *'Mother-Umai,'* who acted as a *'protector of new births and health;'* *Камбар-ата* [qambarata], known as *'Father-Kambar,'* who watched over *horses*; and *Жер-Суу эне* [ʤersüene]' *Mother Nature,* 'who would protect humans from the calamities of the *nature*. There were also other names that we covered in the Volume I.

This journey through divine names weaves the story of our evolving language and our ever-deepening understanding of the world. It showcases evolution of our human capacity to express profound ideas and emotions as we journey through the tapestry of time.

With the advent and widespread use of writing, the initially oral tradition's approach to conveying universally clear and memorable concepts naturally would change. Literacy introduced new possibilities. There was no longer the need to rely solely on memorization for divine names and meanings; instead, they could be tangibly recorded. This transition was akin to the way people today can open their own YouTube channels. Consequently, every major city and even small communities could develop their unique representations of God, much like the ancient practices in Sumer and Egypt or still living ones of India. Simultaneously, the dissemination of the unifying concept of a single God became considerably more manageable.

In summary, the divine terminology is a testament to how early linguistic development within an oral society, deeply connected to the natural world, profoundly shaped the cultural and architectural expressions of later literate urban civilizations. It highlights the enduring impact of nature on our consciousness.

Ancient Consciousness And Nature

As we've explored, the terminology associated with the divine has a deep-rooted connection with the consciousness that developed in humanity's original natural habitats. This connection evolved as human society progressed, particularly with the advent of literacy and the transition to urban environments. Interestingly, even as civilizations became more urbanized, traces of their origins in natural landscapes remained prominent.

Consider, for instance, the Kyrgyz culture, which has a profound connection to its high-altitude mountainous homeland. This connection is reminiscent of the ancient Mesopotamians who frequently depicted the divine realm as the summits of towering mountains on their clay seals. This symbolism was further echoed in the towering hats worn by their deities, known as Tengirs. In ancient Egypt, the connection to mountains was strikingly evident in the form of their pyramids. These monumental structures, initially covered in gleaming white limestone casing stones, bore a striking resemblance to the majestic peaks of mountains.

These cultural symbols hint at the possibility that many early civilizations had their roots in mountainous regions. This observation once again brings to mind the *Inner Asia Mountainous Corridor* theory, which posits that mountainous areas played a pivotal role in the development of human societies and cultures across different parts of the world.

The profound philosophical underpinnings behind the naming of seasons in the prehistoric Kyrgyz calendar are truly awe-inspiring. It is evident that these names emerged from deep contemplation, carrying profound symbolic significance. It features five unique names for its distinct seasons. Each name deeply connected to the philosophical concept of the *eternal life cycle*, the state of *consciousness* (a combination of *awareness* and *senses,* as expressed by the Kyrgyz term *аң-сезим* [aɴ sezim]), and the natural world.

The opening season was called *сары узун* [sarɯuzun], translating to 'the *long yellow*,' encapsulates the transition between late winter and early spring [81]. This period is marked by the presence of yellow snow and grass from the previous year, mirroring the embryonic *'wrinkled'* appearance of a newborn infant and the *'yellow thoughts,'* meaning *сары-санаа* [sarɯ sanä], an *anxiety* for survival. Reminiscent of the critical role of proper nourishment for infants, the most nutritious sustenance, akin to the ingredients of the previously mentioned 'mother's milk-like' dish *малкам* [malqam], is reserved for this season.

The term *жаз* [d͡ʑaz] signifies *spring* in Kyrgyz, the name for the next season. Among other connotations, it carries the idea of (to) *flatten out* and *write,* symbolizing the time of unbending for both nature and consciousness, the time when both start to implement what is written for them by the universe. This is also reflected in the composition of the term as *'Earth/ground* [ʤ] + *high up/top* [a] + *notion of restraint/clench* [z]. 'This combination provides a connotation of a time for *'Earth to open the top after clench,'* reflecting the moment when nature begins to awaken from its slumber, signifying the initial stage of life's renewal.

Following *жаз* is *жай* [ʤaj], which corresponds to the summer months and also translates as (to) *spread*, decoding as time of *'Earth* ([ʤ]) + *opening up* ([a]) + from one to another *end* ([j]). 'This aptly captures the essence of nature's vibrant expansion, evident in the flourishing greenery, abundant pastures, and thriving livestock, aligning with the season of youthfulness.

The term *күз* [gyz] signifies the next season, *fall* in Kyrgyz, and is derived from the same morpheme *'кү'* [qy] as the term *күр* [gyr], which means *high-powered* and *fertile energy*. With the suffix *-з* [z], it symbolizes a finite quality of powerfulness. Consequently, *күз* denotes a season that begins with abundant, fertile energy and matures into fall, marking the end of those qualities. This progression parallels the stages of human life.

Lastly, *кыш* [quʂ], the *winter*, also being an imitative sound signifying *exhaustion*, derives from the same root as, and correspondingly echoes the concept of, *кыс* [qɯs], (to) *clench/squeeze*. By its composition of *'place* ([q]) + *intimate* ([ɯ]) + *together* ([ʂ]) 'the word also denotes *'gathering intimately close together in one place.* 'This term evokes the perception of the season as a time after the fall in energy deteriorated from the preceding season, a time of living "squeezed" in static winter houses, longing for the spaciousness and freedom of the past, the closure of the current life cycle. A "squeezed" or "wrinkled" period, fittingly representing nature's cold months.

The first five months of the year are named after prey animals ("fake" roe, "real" roe, deer, mountain sheep, mountain goat), indicating their peak hunting periods for optimal nutrition [82]. The following two months feature the term to *wallow* (head "wallow" and legs "wallow") hinting at a time of ample rest and leisure, resonating with the youthful spirit and carefree disposition of this stage.

The names of the ensuing months are numerical and are arranged in a descending sequence for the five months of autumn and winter. This arrangement symbolizes the decrease and fading of nature's fertility, mirroring the philosophical concepts of aging and mortality. The sequence commences with *тогуздун айы* [tɒguzdun ajɯ], the *month of nine*. The Kyrgyz word for number "9" [tɒguz] derives from the morpheme *ток* [tɒq] meaning *full*. Accordingly, in Kyrgyz philosophy it symbolizes plenitude. This period roughly corresponds to the end of September and the beginning of October when major celebrations and commemoration events are planned—a time of *fullness in life*.

Subsequently, there is the "month of 7" (mid-October to mid-November), signifying the period when livestock are brought back to their wintering locations and philosophically suggesting a time of settling down.

The "month of 5" (mid-November to mid-December) parallels the concept of aging as winter establishes its dominance.

The month "of 3" (mid-December— mid-January) signifies the harsh winter, reflecting the culmination of life's trials—the final phase in this existence.

Finally, the month "of 1" (mid-January to mid-February) concludes both the calendar year and the philosophical life of the body, representing the symbolical conclusion of one's journey in this world.

The annual cycle comprises 12 years, each named after a specific animal. The year of one's birth within this cycle is deemed crucial and exceptional, inviting elaborate celebrations. During this year, wearing red clothes is customary to attract positive energy, symbolizing *Kut/ Kym* or good fortune. Intriguingly, 19th-century German historian Wilhelm Christian Schott proposed that the Chinese zodiac cycle, named after 12 animals, might have been borrowed from the ancient Kyrgyz people (Schott, 447 in original, 61 in translation). This adds a fascinating cross-cultural dimension to the Kyrgyz calendar's significance.

"THE KYRGYZ ROOTS" OF THE BURNING MAN, ALEXANDER'S IDEAL SOCIETY, AND EGYPTIAN MYTHS

Kyrgyz pre-Soviet culture, predominantly oral, preserved its philosophical wisdom in thousands of sayings and proverbs, forming the bedrock of societal ideology. Functioning as both everyday communication and the main knowledge source, this was an effective form of "neurolinguistic programming" (NLP) to instill ideology within the society via its promotion within the family in the first place.

Caption of the Chapter Opening Image (Fig. 11): Kyrgyz *Komuz* (Source: Public Domain. See List of Figures. Also see Bibliography [Телеканал Баластан @ТелеканалБаластан] for related video on YouTube)

The *komuz*, a fretless stringed instrument, holds a central place in Kyrgyz folk culture. Renowned for its versatility, it can be played in various musical styles, including solo, ensemble, dance accompaniment, and even storytelling.

The custodians of wisdom and advisors to tribal leaders were the assembly of *аксакал* [aqsaqal], the white-bearded seniors mentioned earlier. To grasp the complexity of the "unwritten legislation" that formed the basis for these counselors' way of thinking, consider the collection of over a thousand seven hundred adages only in Academic Yudahin's dictionary archives (Davletbakova, D.), a mere fraction of moral guidelines represented in various folklore forms.

"Begin, Friend, And Set It Up In Your Family" (Plutarch [52])

As the new family is born, among the first wishes given to a young couple was, '*Become an agile old man* (for the groom) *and spry old women* (for the bride)' [53], signifying a wish for the newlyweds to age together in good health—a kind of NLP mantra for a long, happy family life.

Right after, the importance of full respect for the wife and responsibility for her comfort within the new family of husband is instilled in the proverb, '*One who can't make use of silk—turns it to wool, one who can't take thought for the wife—turns her to a bondswoman*' [54].

Continuing this narrative, another adage prioritizes value of a *white headscarf* (attributed to a married woman) over the material wealth (as the ownership of livestock). It sates: '*The first treasure is health, the second treasure is a white headscarf, the third (last) treasure is a hundred of the livestock*' [55] (Devletbakova, 48). The *white headscarf*, representing motherhood and love in general, underscores the pivotal role of women in Kyrgyz families.

Deep love and respect for female family members

commence already from their birth. It symbolized by the mentioned earlier proverb *'The daughter's forty hairs* (traditional hairstyle) *are the seniors of all'* [56], reflecting the girl's place within the family's hierarchy.

This high regard for women continues throughout their lives, evident in the saying, *'If an old man passes away, it frees up the horse; if an old woman does, the place of respect becomes vacant'* [57]. The overall high status of women in pre-Islamic society is also confirmed in the ceremonial tradition of serving the best portion of the meat to the most senior lady, rather than to aksakal.

Parents' unconditional love for their children is expressed through the heartfelt words, *'Let me pass away before you!'* [58]. Simultaneously, proper parenting is a significant part of the nation's ideology, as reflected in the guidance for young couples considering having children —*'A boy grows seeing his father; a girl grows seeing her mother'* [59] —implying that good parenting begets good individuals.

The Kyrgyz society even held fathers accountable for their son's misdeeds, as naughty boys were asked to disclose their father's name for further discussions. This approach, coupled with co-punishment for the father, helped deter crime in the society (Shott, 435 original, 37 translation).

Need for the managing parental unconditional love to ensure proper parenting is further highlighted in the wisdom of folklore. The aqsakal's guidance to the youth emphasizes making the father's name known for good deeds and repaying mother's milk [60]—an idea that solidifies unquestioned respect for seniors in society.

Even family princesses had duties and moral responsibilities, evident in the proverb, *'In a house with a daughter, no fluff lies'* [61], encouraging young girls to contribute to the family's comfort by maintaining cleanliness.

Purity was a crucial concept in ancient Kyrgyz philosophy.

Handwashing before meals is still an important ceremonial act where youngsters pour water for guests, receiving good wishes in return. This also encouraged little boys to serve, ensuring the purity of their intentions.

Cleanliness wasn't just about personal hygiene or household chores but extended to the environment. The guidance *'The place you leave should be purer than the place you arrive'* [62], emphasized the importance of cleaning the seasonal stay place in the semi-nomadic culture.

Purity was integral to a happy life, encapsulated in the fundamental guide: *'A lie cuts short the luck; the dejection cuts down lifespan'* [63] (Davletbakova, 87) highlighting the importance of pure intentions and thoughts for a fortunate, happy life.

Utopias Of Literacy—Echoes Of Orality

Viewing literacy as a technological advancement designed to optimize resource utilization sheds light on the trajectory it set for human progress. Prehistory as seen from the stories of epics, would be of ancient Sumer, Ancient Greeks or Kyrgyz folklore, shown to had far less inclination for the accumulation of wealth than history of literacy has recorded.

A rich Kyrgyz hunter, depicted 1871 by Russian artist as in a picture given in the Volume I, affectionately looking at his bird of prey, *Kyш* [quş], seems had not been interested in filling the interior of his yurt with riches. Also, the adage that encapsulates Kyrgyz folk wisdom, a philosophy that resonates with prehistoric worldviews as confirmed by this book's the research, prioritizes values in the following order: the first is *health*, the second is *love* (symbolized by the *white scarf*) and the only the last of all—material abundance ("a hundred of the livestock"). It underscores the profound emphasis placed on the value of well-being, love for all aspects of existence, and puts least value to riches.

However, literacy ushered in a paradigm shift in the course of human development. While the written word paved the way for the accumulation of material wealth, it inadvertently diverted the collective focus away from the cherished tenets of life in health and with all-encompassing love that had once been paramount.

This dichotomy becomes unmistakably evident in the annals of history, particularly during the tumultuous clashes between the "new" and "old" worlds—a juxtaposition that, once more, emphasizes the influence of the literate mindset. The ramifications of such a divergence are not confined to history alone; contemporary natural disasters and humanitarian crises serve as stark reminders of the complexities that have unfolded due to this redirection.

Furthermore, the root of the dichotomy can be seen to lie in the foundational underpinnings of literate societies—an intricate web woven around the external positioning of oneself within the societal fabric. Here, ego and individual competitiveness stand as defining pillars of the literate society's infrastructure. These principles, while propelling certain advancements, can also foster a disconnect from the communal spirit fostered by orality...

At the same time, in the realm of a literate society, the pursuit of constructing an ideal "right" society has always been a prevailing aspiration. Guided by ideologies reminiscent of Karl Marx's proclamation—*'From each according to his ability, to each according to his needs'*—these aspirations have often carried a utopian essence. This inclination toward a harmonious societal structure can be traced back to our oral heritage, as it inherently values collective well-being and mutual support.

Among these utopian visions, the *Burning Man* project stands out prominently [64]. Despite implementing certain financial regulations to align with the literate world's realities, the essence of the project remains rooted in unearthing the latent capacities of its participants.

Remarkably, the fundamental tenets of this contemporary utopian endeavor strikingly resonate with the societal dynamics of the semi-nomadic, orality-driven Kyrgyz culture of the 19th century, as meticulously documented by the German-Russian historian W. Radlov. Much like in the orality inherent culture described by V. Radlov, the ethos of the *Burning Man* utopia offers all its participants an equal platform to shape and share their expressions, underscoring the enduring value of oral traditions and communal creativity, and lives behind no traces of civilization that can harm nature.

This alignment underscores the persistent presence of certain egalitarian and collective principles that have traversed time, often surviving the transition from primary oral cultures to literate societies. It raises thought-provoking questions about the cyclical nature of societal ideals and the enduring appeal of concepts that champion the balance between individual growth and communal harmony.

An Ideal Society—Alexander's Awakening

In his travelogue about a journey to meet the Kyrgyz people, discussed in Volume I, W. Radlov describes their society as *'dour'* but *'abstaining from plundering.'* He notes that hospitality is sacred to them and that they are all *'invariably the same type of character.'* The *'affluent'* and the '*destitute*' are '*indistinguishable*,' sharing the "*same upbringing and intellectual acumen.*'

Radlov's passage offers a glimpse into a society defined by its commitment to equality and populated by individuals characterized by their integrity and resilience. This portrayal strongly resonates with the image of an ancient civilization, similar to the peaceful society of the prehistoric Indus Valley (also discussed in the Volume I).

Radlov's account also reflects his admiration for the region's musical prowess, folklore, and the dynamic tradition of improvisational singing competitions known as *Айтыш/* aitysh [ajtɯʃ]. While this artistic tradition might not seamlessly transition to the realm of literacy, its enduring presence remains a significant aspect of modern Kyrgyz culture.

Speaking of musical excellence, a particular folk instrument stands out as a guardian of orality—the stringed instrument called *комуз* [qɒmuz] (Refer to the chapter opening image, Fig. 11), which produces resonant sounds when its strings are plucked or struck [65].

Mentioned in BCE records of China [67], this instrument differs from its counterparts by not having frets, which would otherwise confine it to the "box of literacy" with fixed tuning and written musical notation. *Komuz*'s multitude of tunings provides opportunity to produce an endless spectrum of melodies, which is much like orality's broadness compared to the literacy's narrowness framed into the orthography. This unique attribute allows the *komuz* to primarily reside in the realm of improvisation, transcending the boundaries of musical notation and becoming a prominent feature in improvisational singing contests like the *Aitysh*.

The abundance of folk games in Kyrgyz culture, which served as the foundation for the initiation of the *Word*

Nomad Games—"The Olympics" of nomad games—also reflects the profound strength of orality.

One such game is *Тогуз коргоол* [tɒguz-qɒrgɒːl], a two-player intellectual board game meaning '*nine (holes/houses for) small ruminant animal's droppings.*' This game, with its ancient roots, is a fascinating example of a complex strategy game that predates modern computer ones. Players must skillfully maneuver their pieces and secure resources, demonstrating strategic thinking that likely originated from strategies used by our common distant ancestors in their primordial environment.

Fig. 12: T*oguz-korgol* board (Source: Public Domain. See List of Figures)

Toguz-korgool, a strategic board game, takes its name from the Kyrgyz term *korgol*, which literally means *sheep dropping*, reflecting the game's deep connection to pastoral culture. Interestingly, *korgol* can also be translated as *defend yourself* [74], emphasizing the games' intellectual and strategic nature. This dualistic meaning illustrates the "oral mind's" tendency to create names with rich, multi-layered connotations, where all meanings align seamlessly with the intended purpose.

Originally played on the ground, *Тогуз коргоол* is now played on a beautifully crafted board (Fig. 12 above). Each player's side features a larger hole called *the treasury* and nine smaller ones that represent *the houses*. The number *nine* (*Тогуз*) in the game's name, which—as discussed in relation to the names of the months in the Kyrgyz folk calendar—symbolizes abundance, corresponds to these nine *houses*. The term *коргоол* refers the game pieces—originally sheep droppings, now replaced with plastic.

The ancient design of this game, with its holes in the ground and sheep droppings as game pieces, clearly demonstrates the nature-friendly mindset of its ancient creators. This philosophy is also evident in the Kyrgyz saga *Kozhozhash* (See volume I), which teaches that excessive hunting can lead to harsh consequences from Mother Nature.

Moreover, the game's terminology, which includes terms like *коргол* [qɒrgɒl] meaning *ruminant animal's dropping* (which could be collected and pressed into bricks to fuel gentle fires), *казан* [qazan] — *a cooking pot*, and *туз* [tuz] —*the salt*, signifies a process of gathering materials and preparing them for use, without the need for tools or pre-made accessories. This hints at the game's origin in the times of a hunter-gatherer society, the earliest form of human community.

Another intriguing game, *Ordo* (translated as "The General Headquarters"), provides insights into the early counting efforts of our human ancestors. Its unique system, which combines the five fingers of the hand with the intricate use of the phalanges of the four longer fingers (totaling 12), stands as a testament to human ingenuity long before the advent of writing.

As discussed in Volume I, this counting system shares similarities with the ancient Sumerian system. For instance, the number five is expressed by the verbal combination *бирдин учу* [birdin yʨy], which translates to *three of* one, where *one* represents *two visible phalanges of the thumb*, plus *three of the pointing finger*—mirroring the Sumerian method.

In addition to counting objects, the Kyrgyz also used the

12 phalanges of the four longer fingers to count months and years. Interestingly, the numbers in the months' names decrease by two, rather than one, from late summer to the "month of frost." This suggests a possible connection to the thumb, which has only two visible phalanges. By excluding the thumb from the count, the ancient Kyrgyz calendar effectively managed to represent the accelerated pace of nature's decline from late summer to winter, compared to the slower pace of recovery throughout the "yellow long" months of the late winter and early spring.

The ancient Kyrgyz counting system, rooted in finger counting, extended into military terminology. The word for *army*, кол [qol], originates from the word for *hand* [69]. The number of fingers on both hands (ten) provided the basis for structuring military units: 10/ *он* [ɒn] was the fundamental unit, followed by 100/ *жуз* [d͡ʐyz], then 1000/ *миӊ* [miɴ], and finally 10,000/ *түмөн* [tymœn]. Notably, *түмөн* was also used to symbolize the concept of *infinity*.

As a primarily oral culture, Kyrgyz games served as valuable training grounds for military skills. Horse-based games, such as *Көк-бөру* [gœkbœry] (Fig. 13 above), were particularly important. The mass raid version of *Көк-бөру*, *аламан* [alaman], still involves thousands of equestrians (watch YouTube video, see Bibliography – Nurbek Serkebaeev), providing an essential training for cavalry units in ancient Kyrgyz society [70].

Fig. 13: Kok Boru, Kyrgyz Traditional Horse Game (Source: Public Domain. See List of Figures. Also see Bibliography [Nurbek Serkebaev @nurbekserkebaev5714] for reference to the related YouTube video)

The accompanying photograph, taken during the Soviet era, captures the dynamic action of *kok boru*, a traditional Kyrgyz horse game. To fully appreciate the game's unique rules and strategies, viewers are encouraged to watch related videos available on the UNESCO website (see bibliography, UNESCO, 2017).

Hunting with birds of prey and hound dogs was another integral part of Kyrgyz life, both as a sport and a means of subsistence. As evidenced throughout this book, hunting was a significant cultural tradition throughout the history of the Kyrgyz nation...

Interpreting Nizami Ganjavi's 12th-century poem "Eskandar-Nameh"'s [71] reference to *Hirhiz* (Ganjavi, 319) as *Kyrgyz* potentially provides a deeper insight into ancient Kyrgyz society (Ganjavi, 324-339).

Beyond the linguistic connection, the poem's description of a mountainous land north of India and west of China closely aligns with the historical Kyrgyz homeland.

This geographic parallel, along with the depiction of a society that evokes the communal spirit and celebratory nature of modern-day events like Burning Man—when considered alongside Radlov's observations in his time Kyrgyz society (as discussed in Volume I and above)—further strengthens the link between *Hirhiz* and the Kyrgyz people.

The *Eskandar-Name* concludes with a powerful message of wisdom and peace. Alexander the Great, after his global conquests, finds himself in the *Hirhiz* (Kyrgyz) lands, where he finally halts his pursuit of war. This journey culminates in a profound realization: true wisdom and inner peace are not found through military might, but through the simple yet profound teachings of the Kyrgyz people.

Remarkably, the core teaching that the *Hirhiz* elders repeatedly impart to the foreign emperor reflects the lessons my father often shared with me through two proverbs that discussed previously: "*A lie eventually cuts down well-being,*" and "*The first wealth is health, the second is love, and material wealth is only the last.*" The simple yet profound lesson Alexander learns in the celestial *Hirhiz* land is that the true purpose of life is to use one's blessings to create good for others (*Kut*), while living honestly and lovingly...

Connections To Egyptian Mythology

As we explored the possibility of the term *Hirhiz* being connected to *Kyrgyz*, it is also noteworthy to mention that its pronunciations bears resembles to one of the Old Chinese rendering of *Kyrgyz*, *Xiaqiasi* [88]. Given the absence of certain Kyrgyz phonemes in Chinese, substitutions occur: the Kyrgyz *K/g* (which sound like /kh/ or /h/) are replaced with /x/, and *r* is replaced with [a]. By "rewinding" the Chinese transliteration in this way, we can reconstruct a sound that closely resembles *Hirhiz*.

Fig. 14. Symbolic Representation of the Prehistoric Egyptian Deity *Horus*
The image depicts a figure with a human body and the head of a medium-sized hawk, symbolizing the deity *Horus*.

Now, since Greek and Chinese lack the Kyrgyz phoneme [ɯ]—which sounds almost like a "gap" between two consonants pronounced consecutively (try saying *hr*)—it is plausible that some scripts might have recorded the term *Kyrgyz* as *Hrhs*. Similarly, the root word кыр [qɯr] could have been rendered simply as *hr*.

Curiously, the name of the principal deity in prehistoric Egypt, *Horus*, recorded as ḥr.w and depicted in hieroglyphs as a falcon—most likely a *lanner falcon*, renowned for its highly effective hunting practices as a medium-sized raptor [95] (Also see Fig. 14 above).

Based on the logic discussed earlier, we can infer that the original pronunciation may have been close to *hurush* or something similar to the Kyrgyz кырыш [qɯrɯş], which means "annihilation." This concept is explored in the subchapter "Connecting the Dots" concerning the connotations of the term *Kyrgyz* and the co-rooted Kyrgyz names for the *goshawk* and *sparrowhawk*, a medium-sized raptors similar to the *lanner falcon* and known for their prey-annihilating abilities.

It is said that the name of this Egyptian deity later evolved into *Horus*, implying that the original name might have ended with the sound [s] rather than [ş]. Thus, the original pronunciation could be reconstructed as *hurus*, which is strikingly similar to *Kyrgyz*.

Thise and the earlier discussed linguistic connections between Kyrgyz and Ancient Egyptian (explored primarily in Volume I)—such as the name of the Sun God *Ra* and other divine terms, the names associated with the ancient Kingdom of *Kush* in the Upper Nile and with the river itself, the Ancient Egyptian King *Scorpio*, and an ancient tomb in the *Altai* with stone blocks displaying pyramid-like drawings—prompt us to search for further links between the two cultures. Following this line of inquiry, let's add a few more intriguing encounters to the list.

In Egyptian mythology, everything is said to have originated from *Atum*, *tm* [atam], the father of all [93]. In Kyrgyz, we use *Атам* [atam] to mean *my father*.

There is also the deity of negative roles, *Set* or *Seth*, who was the rival of Horus for the people's devotion [90]. The "primeval" structure of this name can be interpreted as '*externally* [s] + *existing* [e] + to the *pantheon* [t]' (referring to a union of the "good gods"). Remarkably, phonetically close words in Kyrgyz reveal strikingly relevant connotations. The Kyrgyz word *сетер* [seter], which has two opposing meanings—*holy* and *riffraff*—features the root *сет* [set] and suffix *-ер* [er] that adds the notion of things '*being in the process of*.' This can be "deciphered" as representing the concept of '*a being of nature* (indicated by "compound" [-er]) that is *external to the union/norm* (expressed by [set]),' signifying a marginalized entity. Additionally, the Kyrgyz word *сес* [ses], meaning *danger*, appears to have been perceived by prehistoric ancestors as '*alien* (external [s] + existence [e]) + *persistently growing* [s].' Collectively, these words paint a unique picture of a being that is both *dangerous* and *marginalized*, yet considered *holy*—aptly reflecting the role of the Egyptian *Set*.

The name *Aha* of the circa 3050 BC pharaoh [91] bears resemblance to the Kyrgyz title *Ага* [aga], which was discussed in connection of the Sumerian Aga of Kish in the first volume of this book.

And the most intriguing connection would be the name *Menes*, believed to be that of the pharaoh who united Ancient Egypt [92]. Interestingly, this name bears a striking resemblance to *Manas*, the name of the hero from the Kyrgyz epic who reunites the nation.

Curiously, when deciphered through the lens of humanity's ur-vocabulary, *Menes* is found to convey a profound philosophical concept: '*self* [m] + *existing* [e] + *object* [n] that *exists* [e] + *infinitely evolving* [s].' This interpretation aligns with the idea of a *Higher Consciousness*, described as "a remarkable western formulation of eastern mystical teaching (of ... no direct knowledge) [94]."

Much like Alexander's quest for the mystical ideal society, this familiar notion of the lost source—"*in the east for the west,*" "*in the west for the east,*" and "*in the north for the south*" (encountered in the Volume I)—can also be strongly linked to the hidden past of the historic Kyrgyz habitat: the *Inner Asian Mountainous Corridor*...

BIBLIOGRAPHY

Bengston, J. (1994). Global Etymologies. ResearchGate, [2018]. [In English]

Chumakeev, E. (2018). Altai-Russian dictionary. PDF document from the Website of Surazakov S.S. Scientific Research Institute.

Darwin, C. (1871). The Descent of Man, and Selection in Relation to Sex. Wordpress.com [In English]

Davletbakova, D. (1997). Sayings and Proverbs of Kyrgyz people: from the collection of academic Yudahin K. (Илим). PDF document from okuma.kg. Website. [In Kyrgyz]

Ganjavi, N. (1194). Eskandar-Name (Translation to Russian by K. Lipsekerova). Чашыоглу, 2007.

Kokboru_YsykKol @kokboru_ysykkol_by_talgat. Салбуурун. Бүркүт салуу. Чыргаа жана үндөө. Nov 13, 2020. [Video].

Radlov, W. (1863). Observations sur les Kirghiz (Translated to Russian by Senilov 1, 19.01.89). PDF document from manusript_Lib.kg. [In Russian]

Schott, W. (1865). Die Ächten Kirgisen (Translation to Kyrgyz by KSU I.Arabaev). Kyrgyz State University, 2020. [In Kyrgyz]

UNESCO. (2017). Kok boru, traditional horse game [Video]. [UNESCO Intangible Heritage, Nomination file No. 01294].

Yudahin, K. (1965). Kyrgyz-Russian Dictionary. (Советская Энциклопедия).

Кара Жорго QARA ZHORGO [@qarajorgo]. 1924 жыл Каркырадагы жарманкеде, кыргыз бийи КАРА ЖОРГО архивны материал. YouTube Video. [dance].

Nurbek Serkebaev @nurbekserkebaev5714. Асманда жылдыз көп,жерде Кыргыз көп Эр Табылды ыры. Mar 30, 2023. [Video].

Телеканал Баластан @ТелеканалБаластан. "Байчечекей" комузчулар ансамбли / "Жаш кербез" / "Талант STAR" долбоору 2021. Jul 28, 2021. [Video].

LIST OF SOURCES FOR IMAGES:

1. "File:Kyrgyz Manaschi, Karakol.jpg." Wikimedia Commons. 15 Jun 2024, 17:58 UTC. 26 Aug 2024, 04:17 <https://commons.wikimedia.org/w/index.php?title=File:Kyrgyz_Manaschi,_Karakol.jpg&oldid=884265282>.

2. "File:Alpine river above Binn VS.jpg." Wikimedia Commons. 3 Aug 2023, 17:03 UTC. 16 Sep 2024, 10:56 <https://commons.wikimedia.org/w/index.php?title=File:Alpine_river_above_Binn_VS.jpg&oldid=789664693>.

3. "File:Юрта в сквере.jpg." Wikimedia Commons. 24 Apr 2022, 18:53 UTC. 28 Aug 2024, 04:58 <https://commons.wikimedia.org/w/index.php?title=File:%D0%AE%D1%80%D1%82%D0%B0_%D0%B2_%D1%81%D0%BA%D0%B2%D0%B5%D1%80%D0%B5.jpg&oldid=651425296>.

4. "File:Calendar aswan.JPG." Wikimedia Commons. 26 Apr 2024, 12:48 UTC. 16 Sep 2024, 10:38 <https://commons.wikimedia.org/w/index.php?title=File:Calendar_aswan.JPG&oldid=871474100>.

5. "File:Dancers on a piece of ceramic from CheshmeAli, Iran, 5000 BC, Louvre.jpg." Wikimedia Commons. 17 Jun 2024, 05:39 UTC. 16 Sep 2024, 09:44 <https://

commons.wikimedia.org/w/index.php?title=File:Dancers_on_a_piece_of_ceramic_from_Cheshme Ali,_Iran,_5000_BC,_Louvre.jpg&oldid=884644124>.

6. "File:Double-alaskan-rainbow.jpg." Wikimedia Commons. 22 Jul 2024, 08:03 UTC. 4 Sep 2024, 11:32 <https://commons.wikimedia.org/w/index.php?title=File:Double-alaskan-rainbow.jpg&oldid=901962245>.

7. "File:Turkey Y chromosome(in 20 haplogroups).png." Wikimedia Commons. 7 Jan 2021, 21:37 UTC. 13 Sep 2024, 09:44 <https://commons.wikimedia.org/w/index.php?title=File:Turkey_Y_chromosome(in_20_haplogroups).png&oldid=524713800>.

8. Screenshots of video from KARA JORGO / КАРА ЖОРГО, @karajorgo2262, retrieved on 06:17 UTC Dec 25, 2023 from https://www.youtube.com/watch?v=N6Rv7a-gjBA.

9. "File:Taigan.jpg." Wikimedia Commons. 17 Nov 2020, 13:30 UTC. 16 Sep 2024, 04:19 <https://commons.wikimedia.org/w/index.php?title=File:Taigan.jpg&oldid=513077341>.

10. "File:KyrgyzEagleHuntsman.jpg." Wikimedia Commons. 31 May 2023, 10:10 UTC. 16 Sep 2024, 12:08 <https://commons.wikimedia.org/w/index.php?title=File:KyrgyzEagleHuntsman.jpg&oldid=768999009>.

11. "File:Girl komuz.JPG." Wikimedia Commons. 18 Aug 2024, 05:45 UTC. 20 Sep 2024, 04:23 <https://commons.wikimedia.org/w/index.php?title=File:Girl_komuz.JPG&oldid=911540931>.

12. "File:Тогузкоргоол.jpg." Wikimedia Commons. 24 Apr 2022, 18:35 UTC. 20 Sep 2024, 04:18 <https://commons.wikimedia.org/w/index.php?title=File:%D0%A2%D0%BE%D0%B3%D1%83%D0%B7%D0%BA%D0%BE%D1%80%D0%B3%D0%BE%D0%BE%D0%BB.jpg&oldid=651422220>.

13. Wikimedia contributors, File:Ulak tartyw.png, retrieved 11:46 UTC Dec 25, 2023 from https://w.wiki/8cjX.

14. "File:God Horus as a falcon wearing the Double Crown of Egypt. 27th dynasty. State Museum of Egyptian Art, Munich.jpg." *Wikimedia Commons*. 5 Jul 2024, 13:11 UTC. 12 Nov 2024, 12:06 <https://commons.wikimedia.org/w/index.php?title=File:God_Horus_as_a_falcon_wearing_the_Double_Crown_of_Egypt._27th_dynasty._State_Museum_of_Egyptian_Art,_Munich.jpg&oldid=892586068>.

NOTES

1. For example, there are words, such as a compound term *айт-буйт* [ajt bujt] (See translation for the word '*айма*'), which consists of prey driving shout (See translation of the word '*айт*,' I), and the imitation for a prompt diving move (See translation of the word '*буйм*'). Neither the compound term nor its stem words were marked by Yudahin as onomatopoeia and correspondingly counted as such by me.

2. https://www.etymonline.com, word '*age (n.)*.'

3. Wikipedia contributors. "Vowel." *Wikipedia, The Free Encyclopedia*. Wikipedia, The Free Encyclopedia, 29 Jul. 2024. Web. 26 Aug. 2024.

4. See translation for the word *ийи* I, II.

5. See translation for the word *ама* II.

6. See translation for the word *э* II.

7. See translation for the word *ээ* II.

8. In Kyrgyz phonology prolonged vowels often turn into the morpheme with the phones [j] or [g] in the middle.

9. [ǂ] as discussed in the Volume I, *Unearthing Our Common Roots* chapter.

10. See translation of the word *шык* II, although to my ear it is closer to the sound [k'].

11. Wikipedia contributors. "Taa language." *Wikipedia, The Free Encyclopedia*. Wikipedia, The Free Encyclopedia, 18 Oct. 2023. Web. 27 Aug. 2024.

12. Wikipedia contributors. "Guttural." *Wikipedia, The Free Encyclopedia*. Wikipedia, The Free Encyclopedia, 30 Jul.

2023. Web. 27 Aug. 2024.

13. Wikipedia contributors. "Ki (goddess)." *Wikipedia, The Free Encyclopedia*. Wikipedia, The Free Encyclopedia, 14 Sep. 2023. Web. 27 Aug. 2024.

14. https://www.etymonline.com, word 'clay (n.)'

15. Wikipedia contributors. "Consonant." *Wikipedia, The Free Encyclopedia*. Wikipedia, The Free Encyclopedia, 20 Aug. 2024. Web. 27 Aug. 2024.

16. Wikipedia contributors. "Samkhya." *Wikipedia, The Free Encyclopedia*. Wikipedia, The Free Encyclopedia, 16 Sep. 2023. Web. 28 Aug. 2024.

17. Wikipedia contributors. "Caesar (title)." *Wikipedia, The Free Encyclopedia*. Wikipedia, The Free Encyclopedia, 25 Aug. 2024. Web. 29 Aug. 2024.

18. https://www.etymonline.com, word '*Sara.*'

19. See translation of the word *кайбар.*

20. See translation of the word *куда* II.

21. https://www.etymonline.com, word '*fore-.*'

22. https://www.etymonline.com, word '*upo.*'

23. "ur-." *Wiktionary*. 11 Oct 2023, 06:01 UTC. 30 Aug 2024, 04:01 <https://en.wiktionary.org/w/index.php?title=ur-&oldid=76312040>.

24. See translation of the word *кут* I, 5.

25. "ἄττα." *Wiktionary*. 1 Dec 2023, 00:03 UTC. 30 Aug 2024, 04:44 <https://en.wiktionary.org/w/index.php?title=%E1%BC%84%CF%84%CF%84%CE%B1&oldid=76827518>.

26. "we." *Wiktionary*. 12 Oct 2023, 06:32 UTC. 30 Aug 2024, 04:46 <https://en.wiktionary.org/w/index.php?title=we&oldid=76317023>.

27. https://www.etymonline.com, word *'me (pron.).'*

28. https://en.wiktionary.org/wiki/Reconstruction:Proto-Indo-European/(s)kelH-.

29. "juxtaposition." *Wiktionary*. 2 Jun 2024, 09:26 UTC. 30 Aug 2024, 05:01 <https://en.wiktionary.org/w/index.php?title=juxtaposition&oldid=79567081>.

30. https://www.etymonline.com, word *'base (adj.).'*

31. https://www.etymonline.com, word *'void (adj.) and void (n.).'*

32. https://www.etymonline.com, word *'gaze (v.).'*

33. https://www.etymonline.com, word *'essence (n.).'*

34. https://www.etymonline.com, word *'cape (n.).*

35. https://www.etymonline.com, word *'captivity (n.).'*

36. Wikipedia contributors. "Zephyrus." *Wikipedia, The Free Encyclopedia*. Wikipedia, The Free Encyclopedia, 27 Jun. 2024. Web. 30 Aug. 2024.

37. "याभ." *Wiktionary*. 1 Nov 2020, 14:39 UTC. 30 Aug 2024, 07:10 <https://en.wiktionary.org/w/index.php?title=%E0%A4%AF%E0%A4%BE%E0%A4%AD&oldid=60996864>.

38. https://en.wiktionary.org/wiki/Reconstruction:Proto-Indo-European/h₃yebʰ-.

39. See translation of the words *адегенде -> де: а дегенде* 1);

40. See translation of the words *ama* II;

41. "ἄγκυρα." *Wiktionary*. 17 Jul 2024, 04:16 UTC. 4 Sep 2024, 11:29 <https://en.wiktionary.org/w/index.php?title=%E1%BC%84%CE%B3%CE%BA%CF%85%CF%81%CE%B1&oldid=80738262>.

42. Wikipedia contributors. "And yet it

moves." *Wikipedia, The Free Encyclopedia.* Wikipedia, The Free Encyclopedia, 30 Jul. 2023. Web. 5 Sep. 2024.

43. Wikipedia contributors. "Human voice." *Wikipedia, The Free Encyclopedia.* Wikipedia, The Free Encyclopedia, 21 Apr. 2024. Web. 6 Sep. 2024.

44. Wikipedia contributors. "Consonant." *Wikipedia, The Free Encyclopedia.* Wikipedia, The Free Encyclopedia, 29 Aug. 2024. Web. 6 Sep. 2024.

45. Wikipedia contributors. "Kurgan hypothesis." *Wikipedia, The Free Encyclopedia.* Wikipedia, The Free Encyclopedia, 11 Oct. 2023. Web. 12 Sep. 2024.

46. https://www.etymonline.com, word 'soul *(n.1).*'

47. Wikipedia contributors. "Xiongnu." *Wikipedia, The Free Encyclopedia.* Wikipedia, The Free Encyclopedia, 12 Nov. 2023. Web. 13 Sep. 2024.

48. Singular, intimate form. The formal and plural is *Арбаңыздар* [arbaɴɯzdar] (Yudahin, 72, *'ары'* III).

49. Wikipedia contributors. "Anu." *Wikipedia, The Free Encyclopedia.* Wikipedia, The Free Encyclopedia, 15 Sep. 2023. Web. 13 Sep. 2024.

50. Wikipedia contributors. "Binomial nomenclature." *Wikipedia, The Free Encyclopedia.* Wikipedia, The Free Encyclopedia, 21 Aug. 2024. Web. 14 Sep. 2024.

51. Wikipedia contributors. "Dog." *Wikipedia, The Free Encyclopedia.* Wikipedia, The Free Encyclopedia, 16 Sep. 2024. Web. 16 Sep. 2024.

52. Wikipedia contributors. "Family as a model for the state." *Wikipedia, The Free Encyclopedia.* Wikipedia, The Free Encyclopedia, 3 Oct. 2023. Web. 17 Sep. 2024.

53. See translation of the word *эбий: Элпилдеген эбий*

бол, алпылдаган абышка бол.

54. See translation of the word *жибек*: *Жибекти туталбаган жүн кылат, катынды күтө албаган күң кылат.*

55. *Биринчи байлык ден-соолук, экинчи байлык ак-жоолук, үчүнчү байлык жүз соолук.*

56. See '*Кыздын кырк чачы улуу.*' See: Wikiquote Contributors, *Кыргыз макал-лакаптар*, information retrieved 06:25 UTC Dec 25, 2023 from https://w.wiki/8EHD.

57. See translation of the word *абышка*: *Абышка өлсө, ат бошойт; кемпир өлсө, төр бошойт.*

58. See translation of the word *алд: алдыңа кетейин.*

59. '*Атаны көрүп уул өсөт, энесин көрүп кыз өсөт*'. See: Wikiquote Contributors, *Кыргыз макал-лакаптар*, information retrieved 10:28 UTC Dec 25, 2023. https://w.wiki/8EHD.

60. '*Атанын атын чыгарган, эненин сүтүн актаган бала бол!*'

61. '*Кызы бар үйдө кыл жатпайт.*' See: Wikiquote Contributors, *Кыргыз макал-лакаптар*, information retrieved 10:29 Dec 25, 2023 from https://w.wiki/8EHD.

62. See translation of the word *аруу*" I, 1: *Келген жериңден кеткен жериң аруу болсун!*

63. '*Калп ырысты кесет, кайгы өмүрдү кесет.*'

64. Wikipedia contributors. "Burning Man." *Wikipedia, The Free Encyclopedia*. Wikipedia, The Free Encyclopedia, 29 Sep. 2023. Web. 17 Sep. 2024.

65. Wikipedia contributors. "Komuz." *Wikipedia, The Free Encyclopedia*. Wikipedia, The Free Encyclopedia, 19 May. 2023. Web. 17 Sep. 2024.

66. "File:One Kyrgyz Som-(detail).jpg." *Wikimedia Commons.* 4 Sep 2023, 14:45 UTC. 17 Sep 2024, 07:56 <https://commons.wikimedia.org/w/index.php?title=File:One_Kyrgyz_Som-(detail).jpg&oldid=798399795>.

67. "Комуз (струнный музыкальный инструмент)". *Wikipedia, the free encyclopedia.* 25 March 2024, 11:03 UTC. 18 September 2024, 02:09 <https://ru.wikipedia.org/?curid=13819&oldid=130656472>.

68. Wikipedia contributors. "Toguz korgol." *Wikipedia, The Free Encyclopedia.* Wikipedia, The Free Encyclopedia, 5 Mar. 2024. Web. 19 Sep. 2024.

69. See translation of the word *кол* II.

70. "Кок-бору". *Wikipedia, the free encyclopedia.* 17 September 2024, 07:09 UTC. 20 September 2024, 06:09 <https://ru.wikipedia.org/?curid=4071013&oldid=140252472>.

71. Wikipedia contributors. "Nizami Ganjavi." *Wikipedia, The Free Encyclopedia.* Wikipedia, The Free Encyclopedia, 20 Sep. 2024. Web. 8 Oct. 2024.

72. Wikipedia contributors. "Bashkirs." *Wikipedia, The Free Encyclopedia.* Wikipedia, The Free Encyclopedia, 30 Sep. 2024. Web. 8 Oct. 2024.

73. See translation of the word *ар* IV, V and VI.

74. See translation of the words *корго* and *корголо.*

75. See translation of the word *жай* II, 4: *аркы жай.*

76. https://www.etymonline.com, word '*archon (n.).*'

77. "arc." *Wiktionary.* 27 Sep 2024, 11:28 UTC. 9 Oct 2024, 08:51 <https://en.wiktionary.org/w/index.php?title=arc&oldid=81969814>.

78. Wikipedia contributors. "Beer yoga." *Wikipedia, The*

Free Encyclopedia. Wikipedia, The Free Encyclopedia, 25 Mar. 2023. Web. 21 Oct. 2024.

79. See how some languages have many words for color white, including Sanskrit: Wikipedia contributors. "White." *Wikipedia, The Free Encyclopedia.* Wikipedia, The Free Encyclopedia, 5 Oct. 2024. Web. 21 Oct. 2024. [section *Etymology*]. Also check the online dictionary: https://sanskritdictionary.com.

80. Wikipedia contributors. "Ancient Egyptian religion." *Wikipedia, The Free Encyclopedia.* Wikipedia, The Free Encyclopedia, 18 Oct. 2024. Web. 22 Oct. 2024.

81. See translation of the word *сары* I, *узун сары*.

82. See translation of the word *ай* I, 2).

83. Wikipedia contributors. "Vṛddhi." *Wikipedia, The Free Encyclopedia.* Wikipedia, The Free Encyclopedia, 13 Sep. 2024. Web. 29 Oct. 2024.

84. Wikipedia contributors. "Obstruent." *Wikipedia, The Free Encyclopedia.* Wikipedia, The Free Encyclopedia, 25 Feb. 2024. Web. 4 Nov. 2024.

85. Wikipedia contributors. "Click consonant." *Wikipedia, The Free Encyclopedia.* Wikipedia, The Free Encyclopedia, 27 Oct. 2024. Web. 4 Nov. 2024.

86. Wikipedia contributors. "List of animal sounds." *Wikipedia, The Free Encyclopedia.* Wikipedia, The Free Encyclopedia, 28 Oct. 2024. Web. 4 Nov. 2024.

87. See translations of the word *ық* III and VI. Also note that other given translation for this word actually correspond to very similar but different words. The meaning under the number I corresponds to the term *нық*, under II to *дық*, IV *ықтыт*, V to *ыдық*.

88. Wikipedia contributors. "Khakas." *Wikipedia, The*

Free Encyclopedia. Wikipedia, The Free Encyclopedia, 5 Nov. 2024. Web. 12 Nov. 2024.

89. Wikipedia contributors. "Horus." *Wikipedia, The Free Encyclopedia*. Wikipedia, The Free Encyclopedia, 10 Nov. 2024. Web. 12 Nov. 2024.

90. Wikipedia contributors. "Set (deity)." *Wikipedia, The Free Encyclopedia*. Wikipedia, The Free Encyclopedia, 23 Oct. 2024. Web. 12 Nov. 2024.

91. Wikipedia contributors. "Hor-Aha." *Wikipedia, The Free Encyclopedia*. Wikipedia, The Free Encyclopedia, 26 Sep. 2024. Web. 12 Nov. 2024.

92. Wikipedia contributors. "Menes." *Wikipedia, The Free Encyclopedia*. Wikipedia, The Free Encyclopedia, 29 Oct. 2024. Web. 12 Nov. 2024.

93. Wikipedia contributors. "Atum." *Wikipedia, The Free Encyclopedia*. Wikipedia, The Free Encyclopedia, 15 Oct. 2024. Web. 12 Nov. 2024.

94. Wikipedia contributors. "Higher consciousness." *Wikipedia, The Free Encyclopedia*. Wikipedia, The Free Encyclopedia, 25 Oct. 2024. Web. 12 Nov. 2024.

95. Wikipedia contributors. "Lanner falcon." *Wikipedia, The Free Encyclopedia*. Wikipedia, The Free Encyclopedia, 2 Nov. 2024. Web. 12 Nov. 2024.

ABOUT THE AUTHOR

Shaktybek Imashov

Driven by a fascination with yoga's prehistoric roots, I embarked on the creation of the Proto-Yoga series.

My unique perspective is shaped by a diverse background, encompassing international management consultancy, Soviet-era education in Russian language, and deep immersion in Kyrgyz culture. This blend enables me to navigate the intricacies of Kyrgyz folklore and linguistics, analyze primary sources in English, Russian, and Kyrgyz, and explore the wide-ranging topics covered in the three volumes.

Beyond scholarly exploration, my goal was to translate these findings into practical application. I integrated postures, stretches, mantras, body vibrations, and meditation inspired by the fusion of yoga and Kyrgyz cultural elements into my daily routine. This unique Kyrgyz form of Proto-Yoga will be detailed in the final volume of the series, currently in development.

To complement the written exploration, I plan to launch a dedicated YouTube channel, where I will delve deeper into the movements, mantras, and other techniques of this fascinating "primordial tradition of the common humanity."

Printed in Dunstable, United Kingdom